Jitters

JITTERS

a play by David French

Talonbooks . Vancouver . Los Angeles . 1980

copyright ©1980 David French

published with assistance from the Canada Council

Talonbooks   Talonbooks
201 1019 East Cordova   P.O. Box 42720
Vancouver   Los Angeles
British Columbia V6A 1M8   California 90042
Canada   U.S.A.

This book was typeset by Linda Gilbert, designed by
David Robinson and printed by Webcom for Talonbooks.

First printing: April 1980

Talonplays are edited by Peter Hay.

Jitters was first published by Playwrights Co-op, Toronto,
Ontario.

Canadian Cataloguing in Publication Data

French, David, 1939—
        Jitters

        ISBN 0-88922-170-7

        I. Title.
    PS8561.R45J5 1980   C812'.54   C80-091169-5
    PR9199.3.F75J5 1980

to Sean Sullivan

Jitters was first performed at Tarragon Theatre in Toronto, Ontario on February 16, 1979, with the following cast:

Patrick	David Calderisi
Jessica	Charmion King
Phil	Les Carlson
George	Miles Potter
Robert	Matt Walsh
Tom	Jim Mezon
Nick	Morison Bock
Susi	Amanda Lewis
Peggy	Sheilah Currie

Directed by Bill Glassco
Designed by David Moe
Lighting by Robert Thompson

Jitters was also performed at the Long Wharf Theatre in New Haven, Connecticut on October 16, 1979, with the following cast:

Patrick:	Roland Hewgill
Jessica	Charmion King
Phil	George Sperdakos
George	Jim Jansen
Robert	Josh Clark
Tom	Joel Polis
Nick	William Carden
Susi	Jane Galloway
Peggy	Sarah Chodoff

Directed by Bill Glassco
Designed by Eldon Elder
Costumes by Rachel Kurland
Lighting by Jamie Gallagher

The Characters

Patrick Flanagan, 50
Jessica Logan, 50
Phil Mastorakis, 44
George Ellsworth, 30
Robert Ross, 26
Tom Kent, 22
Nick, 28
Susi, 23
Peggy, 20

Act One

An afternoon in May

Act Two

Four days later

Act Three

The next afternoon

Act One

The set is the set of a play-within-a-play, although the audience is as yet unaware of this. It is the living room of a middle-class home. Night. There is a sofa, an armchair, a hi-fi, hanging plants and a Christmas tree. In the hallway, a staircase leads up to the second floor. The front door is offstage.

At rise, JESSICA is seated on the sofa, knitting with the sort of concentration that is an attempt to hide anxiety.

At the table, PHIL and TOM have just finished a hand of gin. While TOM shuffles the cards, PHIL pours himself a glass of scotch.

PHIL: *to JESSICA*   It's almost midnight. I don't think he'll be back. . . . Can I get you something?

JESSICA does not respond.

PHIL: Hey, Sis, I heard a good story this week. There were these two trappers in a log cabin . . .

JESSICA: *cutting in* Eric, you don't have to amuse me, I'm quite all right.

TOM hurls the cards down on the table and rises.

TOM: Oh, for Christ's sake, mother!

He crosses stage left and stands shuffling his feet.

JESSICA: Watch your language, you. I won't have that sort of language in this house.

TOM: That's funny, coming from you.

JESSICA: When have you heard me talk like that? I have never used that sort of language. Ever.

TOM: No, but Frank does.

JESSICA: He can do what he wants in this house. That's something you don't seem to understand. Well, accept it or get out. I have my own life now, and I won't have you interfering.

PHIL: That's not fair, Elizabeth.

TOM: I don't want you making a fool of yourself. The man's an opportunist.

JESSICA: Aren't we all? You think I'm any better? If you do, you better go back to school.

PHIL: I think what Jimmy means. . . .

JESSICA: *cutting in* I know what he means, you don't have to translate. *To TOM.* Well, maybe he is an opportunist. So what? He's had to crawl out of a life you only know from books. You better be sure you know what you're talking about before you pass judgement on others. That goes for you, too, Eric. Of all people, you ought to know better.

*The front door slams. JESSICA springs to her feet, calling
"Frank?" Clutching her knitting, she rushes to the hallway
and stops as PATRICK enters. He glances around, then at
JESSICA. He mutters "Lizzie" and moves into her embrace.
Then he steps to the hatrack and mimes taking off his hat
and coat. At that moment, GEORGE jumps up from his
aisle seat in the audience.*

GEORGE: Cut. That's terrific. We'll stop there. We'll
    run it from the top now in costume.

PATRICK: Christ, I just get my hat and coat off. . . .

*PEGGY enters from backstage and begins to set up for the
top of the play.*

GEORGE: How was that, Jess? Did the knitting help?

JESSICA: It's perfect. Exactly the sort of thing a woman
    might do if she's anxious.

GEORGE: You sure, love?

JESSICA: Absolutely. I've done it myself: cleaned the
    oven, waxed the floor.

PATRICK: Just don't get too excited when you rush
    out to greet me. I don't want a knitting needle in my eye.

He sits on the sofa.

JESSICA: Don't worry about me. Worry more about
    the critics. They go straight for the jugular without
    dropping a stitch.

She exits backstage.

TOM: How's my position, George? It always feels . . .
    you know . . . like I'm too far stage left.

GEORGE: No, I want the distance. Only don't shuffle your feet. It looks like you're doing a soft shoe.

TOM: I'm expressing my anxiety.

PATRICK: Why don't you have him clean the oven or wax the floor?

GEORGE: Tom, it's better to remain still. Especially when Jess is speaking. At that moment the focus should be on her and you take it away if you move.

PATRICK: *to TOM*   In other words, you're upstaging our star. Cut it out.

TOM: *to GEORGE*   I won't do it again. I promise. Thanks.

He gestures playfully to PATRICK.

PATRICK: Get away or I'll spank you.

TOM: Biggest scene stealer of all time.

He exits.

GEORGE starts down the aisle.

NICK: *over the P.A.*   A run-through of the show will begin in twenty minutes. Please be ready to go at four o'clock. Peggy, be set as soon as you can.

PHIL: George, old buddy, have you seen my costume? My so-called costume?

GEORGE: *stepping onstage*   What's wrong with it?

PHIL: It's hideous. I'm insulted. Deeply offended.

GEORGE: Put it on, Phil. Let's have a look.

He sits down at the table and takes a sandwich out of his lunchbag.

PHIL: George, you're a wonderful man, a sweetheart. I'd do anything for you. Anything. Even take my shirt off on stage. But don't ask me to be more ridiculous than that.

He exits backstage.

PATRICK: I'm waiting. And don't tell me again she didn't mean it. That's the second time in two days.

GEORGE: *eating his sandwich*   I still think it was an accident.

PATRICK: Don't give me that. The apron is supposed to hit my chest, not my face. She threw it so hard it knocked my hat off.

GEORGE: That part I don't like. But your reaction was marvellous.

PATRICK: What reaction?

GEORGE: The way you raised your fist.

PATRICK: That was my own reaction, not the character's.

GEORGE: Keep it. And I loved that little dance you did. Like you were holding the lid on a volcano.

PATRICK: That wasn't *acting*, mate. I wanted to punch her in the mouth. Knock her right on her twelve-carat ass.

GEORGE: Patrick, the tension was terrific. I wasn't sure whether you were going to hit her or not. Believe me, the audience will feel that, too.

PATRICK: I'll let you in on a little secret. You listening?
If she throws that apron in my face one more time, I
won't leave you or the audience in any doubt. Is that too
subtle for you?

Enter SUSI with a sewing basket.

SUSI: George, treasure, I hate to interrupt but since I'm
such a good sport I've volunteered to work on my tea
break.

GEORGE: What is it, Susi?

PATRICK: God, isn't she lovely?

SUSI: The sofa cushion needs mending. Would you mind if
I did it now? I'm in a hurry.

GEORGE: Now or later, love. But it has to be done by
tonight.

PATRICK rises and crosses to the table.

GEORGE: Sorry. Where were we?

SUSI sits on the sofa and mends the cushion.

PATRICK: We were talking about that prima donna.
Canada's own Jessica Logan. God, that kills me. One or
two hit plays on Broadway, and suddenly she's a national
resource.

GEORGE: You want a sandwich?

PATRICK: Even in that Albee piece she played herself.
That's all she can do, bitches.

GEORGE: I made it myself. Cheddar cheese on
pumpernickel.

14

PATRICK: Bitches and tarts. That's her forte. Middle-aged bitches and sleazy tarts.

GEORGE: Pat, she's not playing a bitch. This is a very sympathetic role.

PATRICK: And smaller than mine. And for that she gets top billing. I have to squint to read my name on the posters.

GEORGE: Look, I know you two aren't exactly hitting it off, but your work together is sensational. I'm very happy. So is Robert.

PATRICK: Well, he has a funny way of showing it. Most days he slinks in here and broods. His silences are right out of Pinter.

GEORGE: He's just shy. It's only his second play.

PATRICK: Today's the first time he's spoken to me all week. Come to think of it, I prefer his silences. No, really, he has no tact, that kid. So keep him away from me. As far as possible.

PHIL: *off* George, I'm dressed. Are you ready for this?

GEORGE: Just a minute, Phil. *To PATRICK.* Look, we'll talk about this later, okay?

PATRICK: I'm a damned fine actor, and he ought to consider himself lucky to get me. Instead he picks away at my confidence. Well, this's the last play of his I'm ever going to do, and you can tell him that for me.

He exits backstage.

SUSI: *still mending the cushion* He's really on the warpath, isn't he? I'm glad I kept my mouth shut.

PEGGY: That's the first time he's attacked Robert. I'm surprised.

GEORGE: Well, it's the first preview tonight. That might have something to do with it.

PHIL: *off*   George, I'm still here. I haven't got all day.

GEORGE: Whenever you're ready.

PHIL enters, dressed as a priest.

PHIL: Well?

GEORGE: You look great. What's the problem?

PHIL: Are you kidding? Look how tight the pants are. The man's a priest, not a flamenco dancer. What priest wears tight pants? Not only is it sacrilegious, it's worse — it's ludicrous.

GEORGE: They don't look that tight.

PHIL: No, not if I'm dancing *Swan Lake*. George, old buddy, this is a contemporary play. You want me in this costume? Fine. Give me a rapier and change my lines to iambic pentameter.

GEORGE: How is it otherwise?

PHIL walks around and lifts his jacket.

PHIL: See for yourself. Not only are the pants tight, they're shiny. Is this man so poor he has to iron his own pants?

GEORGE: Is that it?

PHIL: No, this clerical collar's too small. I've got a 15½ neck, the collar's 14. We've got four previews, George. Four previews starting tonight. By the opening my eyes'll bug out so much they'll think I have a thyroid condition.

GEORGE: *wearily* What else, Phil?

PHIL: Isn't that enough?

GEORGE: All right, I'll see what I can do. Thanks.

PHIL: *as he starts to exit* I won't even mention the shoes.

GEORGE: What's wrong with the shoes?

PHIL: *stops* The right one pinches.

GEORGE: Why just the right?

PHIL: My right foot's one inch longer than my left. *He points at SUSI.* And no jokes.

GEORGE: All right. I'll talk to Wardrobe, they must've forgotten. We don't want you mincing in this role.

PHIL: And one last thing, George. Bear with me on this.

GEORGE: What?

PHIL: Believe me, I don't want to be difficult. I hesitate to even mention it, it's the hairpiece. I ask you, what priest wears a toupée?

SUSI: A priest with tight pants.

PHIL: *to GEORGE* You see that? From the mouth of babes, George. From the mouth of babes. *To SUSI.* Thank you, sweetheart.

GEORGE: Listen, I was against the hairpiece from the start. It was your idea.

PHIL: Okay, so I changed my mind. It looks tacky. Besides, who the hell needs a rug? I can *act* hair!

He exits backstage.

SUSI: He's making the girls in Wardrobe rich. They've never had so much overtime.

GEORGE: *to the control booth*   Nick, did you get all that?   *Then.*   Nick?

PEGGY: He may have gone for a coffee.

GEORGE: Then tell Wardrobe to take Phil's pants away for the run-through.

PEGGY: There's nothing wrong with his pants.

GEORGE: I know that, but let him think they've been worked on. He'll drive us crazy, otherwise.

He has finished eating. He crumples the paper bag and tosses it off the stage.

Enter TOM.

TOM: Susi, do you think I could have two comps for tomorrow night? My dad can't make the opening.

SUSI: No problem. I'll leave two tickets at the box office in your name. How's that?

TOM: Great. Thanks.

SUSI: And next time you want a favour, Tom, drop by my apartment. We'll talk about it in the shower.

TOM: Is she kidding, George? I'll never know when she's kidding.

PEGGY: She's not kidding, Tom. Her water bill's higher than her rent.

SUSI: Claws in, angel.

GEORGE: Let's skip hygiene for now, Tom. Sit down. *TOM does.*   Tell me, how's Jess?

TOM: Oh, I think she's a fabulous actress. She's so easy to work with . . .

GEORGE: *cutting in*   No, I mean how's she holding up? It's hard to know with Jess. Did she say anything at lunch?

TOM: She's not showing it, George, but she's really upset. Like, she kept dropping her knife and fork. Things like that.

GEORGE: What else?

TOM: She wouldn't eat her sandwich. Luigi made it with mayonnaise and she made him take it back. Jess never complains like that, even when the toast is burnt.

SUSI: Is Patrick still calling her at three in the morning?

TOM: Yeah, he is. I told her she should take her phone off.

PEGGY: And did she?

TOM: Yeah, she did. And two nights running he called the guy next door. He said it was an emergency, her phone was off the hook, and could he run next door and tell her.

GEORGE: *rising*   Jesus, he's impossible.

19

TOM: I know. Now the guy next door has *his* phone off the hook. So like, last night, guess what happens?

GEORGE: What?

TOM: Around three or four in the morning, she said, a pizza truck pulls up in front of her house.

GEORGE: A pizza truck?

TOM: She says if he gets any more smart ideas and sends an ambulance, she'll go him one better and take it. Then he'll be up a creek.

SUSI: Won't we all?

GEORGE: Okay, thanks, Tom. You better finish dressing.

TOM is staring at SUSI.

GEORGE: Tom.

TOM: Oh. You bet.

He jumps up and exits.

NICK: *over the P.A.*   Peggy, have you finished your preset?

PEGGY: George, is that where you want the armchair? You better double check. Yes, Nick, we're all set.

GEORGE: *to PEGGY*   That's perfect. Would you tell the cast I want to speak to them onstage before the run-through? And tell Jess and Patrick to come out as soon as they're ready. I need them for a minute or two.

PEGGY: I'll hurry them up.

GEORGE: One more thing. Any sign of a bottle?

PEGGY shakes her head.

GEORGE: Keep checking the dressing room. If you find anything, let me know. I'll handle it.

PEGGY: Actors who drink make me nervous.

SUSI: Actors who drink and make phone calls at three a.m. make me glad I'm front-of-house. I wouldn't want to be on stage with one.

PEGGY: I like Patrick, though. I know he's a bastard, but he's very sensitive.

She exits backstage.

SUSI: Oh, God, not one of those types. Is she in the right business. There. I'm finished, George. Anything else I can do?

GEORGE: Yes, I want you on book for the run-through. Robert's been bitching again. He's worried about the text.

SUSI: George, I don't have all that much time. I still have to clean the lobby and washrooms.

GEORGE: Get one of the other girls to do that. This is more important. The actors really are getting sloppy. If they aren't reminded, they'll get locked into it. Phil is the worst.

SUSI: I can believe that. I've been running lines with him. I know them better than he does.

GEORGE: How's the house?

SUSI: We're sold out. A waiting list of eighteen, last time I checked. And the word from New York is good. Bernie Feldman is definitely coming.

GEORGE: His office confirmed it?

SUSI: This morning. He'll be here for the opening. So cheer up, treasure. We just might be making headlines.

She exits.

GEORGE: *to the control booth* Nick, are you in the booth?

NICK: *over the P.A.* I'm here.

GEORGE: Good. I want to make a change in the sound level at the top of the show. It's too loud. What is it now?

NICK: It's at four.

GEORGE: Bring it down to three and a half. You got that?

NICK: Yeah, I got it.

GEORGE: And I want the music in faster. As soon as the house goes to half, bring it in and up. Don't wait.

NICK: I wish you'd make up your mind. This morning you told me to go to black before I bring in the music.

GEORGE: That's what run-throughs are for, Nick. So I can change my mind. I may even change it again before we open. Now, did you get that? *Then.* Nick?

NICK: What? The new cue or the sarcasm?

ROBERT enters down the aisle, carrying two cups of coffee in styrofoam cups.

GEORGE: Oh, hi, Robert. I thought you'd left.

ROBERT: *suspiciously* Why? Did you want me to?

GEORGE: No, of course not. Listen, did you say anything to Patrick today? Anything that might upset him?

He takes a coffee.

ROBERT: I said hello, that's all. Why? Did he say I upset him?

GEORGE: No, but he's got this idea in his head you don't like what he's doing. I thought maybe you knew why.

ROBERT: Jesus, I think it's the best thing he's ever done. I couldn't be more pleased. I love to come in here and just watch him work.

GEORGE: Don't tell me, tell him.

ROBERT: I couldn't.

GEORGE: Why not?

ROBERT: I couldn't say things like that to his face, I'd be too embarrassed. Besides, it's Jess I'm worried about. She was terrible today.

GEORGE: I know. All of a sudden she's playing emotions instead of objectives.

ROBERT: What're you going to do about it?

GEORGE: Well, it's only been the last couple of days. I'll see what happens in the run-through. Meanwhile, do me a favour: stay out of his way; don't even look at him.

ROBERT: Yeah, and then he'll think for sure I don't like him.

GEORGE: Now you know what I go through. If I spend too much time with Jess, he says I'm neglecting him. If I do give him special attention, he gets insecure and says, "Why don't you work with her? She's the one who needs it."

ROBERT: Be firm. You're the director. Either he gets his act together . . .

GEORGE: *cutting in* Or what? If I lay down the law, he might quit. It's four days to opening. You want that? *ROBERT says nothing.* He knows damn well we can't replace him. He thinks he can pull any stunt now and get away with it.

ROBERT: That's even more reason to be firm, isn't it? What if Jess decides she can't take any more? What then?

GEORGE: She won't.

ROBERT: How do you know?

GEORGE: She's no fool, Jess. He may be difficult, but he gives her a lot to work with. The best scenes in the play are the ones they have together.

ROBERT: *defensively* They also happen to be the best-written.

GEORGE: I'm not saying they're not. All I'm saying is this play could be her ticket back to New York and she knows it. Why do you think she dragged Feldman up to Toronto? Why do you think she's letting Patrick get away with so much?

Enter JESSICA followed by PATRICK. She is now wearing a curly blonde wig.

JESSICA: George, I want your unbiased opinion. Does this wig look funny?

GEORGE: It doesn't look funny. It looks stunning.

PATRICK: *to JESSICA*   I never said the wig looked funny. I said you looked funny in the wig. Hello, Robert. Still waiting to see if I improve?

JESSICA: He'll have to wait a helluva long time if your wit is any indication of your talent.   *To GEORGE.* What can we do for you, darling? Peggy said you wanted to see us.

NICK: *over the P.A.*   Top of Act One in five minutes, please.

GEORGE: I want to go over a moment in the second act. There seems to be a slight problem.

JESSICA: What moment's that?

GEORGE: The bit with the apron.

PATRICK: Oh, *that* moment.

JESSICA: I thought that moment worked quite well for me.

PATRICK: I think that's the problem.

GEORGE: I just don't want anyone to get hurt. So let's take a look at it. Jess, are you hitting your mark?

JESSICA: I always hit my mark.

PATRICK: Notice how she looks my way? Try to be a little more subtle, love. In the trade we call that "indicating."

JESSICA: Yes, I know. I saw your Shylock.

GEORGE: What about you, Patrick? It seems to me you were a little too far upstage of the table.

PATRICK: Well, I hate to contradict the director, but I was standing exactly where I always stand.

GEORGE: Okay, let's see your positions. That way I can judge for myself.

He goes up the aisle.

PATRICK and JESSICA take their positions upstage of the table.

PATRICK: Here it is. I haven't budged since we blocked it.

GEORGE: Are you in position, Jess?

JESSICA: I am.

TOM rushes on, dressed in yellow polo pajamas.

TOM: Do you need me, George? Peggy said you were doing the "apron scene."

GEORGE: No, I don't need you, Tom. Thanks, anyway.

TOM exits.

GEORGE: Patrick, maybe if you moved a step or two closer, she'd be more certain of her aim.

PATRICK: If it's a question of aim, I'd prefer to move back if you don't mind.

JESSICA: Aren't you being paranoid? It was an accident.

PATRICK: Listen, that was no accident. Once is an accident. Twice is assault with intent to wound. Is that the best you could dream up, an apron in the face?

JESSICA: No, but then it's not four in the morning, is it? Which reminds me. Next time you order pizza, make it a small without anchovies.

PATRICK: What're you talking about?

JESSICA: And call the same place. I adored that curly-haired delivery boy.

PATRICK: I don't know what she's talking about. She's crazy.

GEORGE: Please, Jess, Patrick, the moment's not that important. *To JESSICA.* From now on just toss the apron at his feet. That'll make the same point.

ROBERT reacts to this.

PATRICK: Fine, but I won't pick it up.

GEORGE: I'm not asking you to. Tom's in the scene, I'll have him pick it up.

ROBERT: Wait a minute, George. Don't you think that weakens the moment? It's much stronger if she hits him.

PATRICK: *to ROBERT* Listen, boy, one moment's not going to make or break your precious play, so don't get defensive. I don't care what the script says, I'm not getting an apron snapped in my face. Is that understood?

He exits.

JESSICA: Adamant, isn't he? That's what I like, a man who knows what he doesn't want. *To ROBERT.* Give me a cigarette, darling.

ROBERT does, and lights it for her. She inhales deeply.

JESSICA: *as GEORGE comes down the aisle and steps on the stage*   Don't worry: no more aprons in the face. I've gotten it out of my system. But God, it felt good. I could've done that all day.

ROBERT: I don't blame you.

JESSICA: *sits at the table*   What was he like in *Murphy's Diamond*? Was he much trouble?

ROBERT: No, but he had top billing, remember. And he always gets along with . . .   *He stops, realizing he's almost put his foot in his mouth.*   . . . you know . . . with. . . .

He looks to GEORGE for help.

JESSICA: With what? Young actors?

GEORGE: *quickly*   Actors like Tom. Kids he doesn't feel threatened by. You know.   *He gives ROBERT a look.*   Pat's getting a reputation for being temperamental. He'd better watch out or no one'll hire him.

JESSICA: Don't kid yourself. Any actor as good as Flanagan always works. But never mind about him. How am *I* doing? I can't tell anymore. I don't feel I'm doing justice to the woman.

GEORGE: It's coming along beautifully. Isn't it, Robert? God, the improvement today in the second act was phenomenal. It's not quite there yet, granted, but you have no need to worry.

JESSICA: I've been away two years, George. I'm rusty. I can't seem to relax and enjoy it.

GEORGE: You tell her, Robert. She's wonderful, isn't she?

ROBERT: It's a much tougher role than Flanagan's. He has the far more colourful character.

JESSICA: Oh? You think so?

GEORGE: I think what Robert means is that you're very close to this character and that's hard to play. Whereas Patrick's role is a character role. Isn't that what you meant, Robert?

ROBERT: Yeah. Right.

JESSICA: Why don't you let him speak for himself?

Enter PHIL and TOM.

PHIL: Here we are, friends. "The brief abstracts and chroniclers of our time."

TOM: What's that from?

PHIL: *Hamlet.*

TOM: Did you do *Hamlet*?

PHIL: Are you kidding? I've done all the classics.

TOM: Who'd you play, Osric?

PHIL: No, the gravedigger.

GEORGE: Don't believe him. He did the Player Queen and he was damn good, too. He only did the gravedigger one night. Where's Patrick?

PATRICK: *entering*   Coming.

PATRICK sits at the table. PEGGY enters and also sits at the table. JESSICA and TOM sit on the sofa. PHIL moves to the armchair and ROBERT to the window seat. GEORGE remains on his feet.

NICK: *over the P.A.*   George, we have two and a half hours to have this run. If you want the actors to have a proper dinner break, we have to start right away.

GEORGE: *to the control booth*   This'll only take two
   minutes.

NICK: We don't have two minutes.

GEORGE: Then we'll make two minutes, won't we? . . .
   Okay, let's settle down. I just want to say a few words.
   First, I think you'll all agree we made enormous progress
   today with Act Two. Some exciting things were
   beginning to happen. I know you all felt that.   *Slight
   pause.*   You did all feel that, didn't you? I thought
   the last scene was stupendous. It still needs toning
   down, but it was really beginning to cook.

PHIL: George, I still don't have the new shoes. Have you
   spoken to Wardrobe?

GEORGE: No, I haven't had time. I promise you'll have
   them for tonight. Peggy, make a note of that. Phil has to
   have new shoes.   *To the control booth.*   Nick,
   did you hear that?

NICK: *over the P.A.*   What size?

PHIL: A nine and a ten.

NICK: Come again.

GEORGE: He needs two different sizes. One foot's a bit
   longer than the other.   *To PHIL.*   Actually, you only
   need one shoe, don't you? The left foot?

PHIL: No, the right.   *To NICK.*   A size ten for the
   right foot, sweetheart. And make sure they match. I
   don't want the audience staring at my feet.

30

GEORGE: Okay, let's go on. Where was I? . . . Oh, yeah. Right now the show's running at least ten minutes too long. We can slash five minutes off tonight just by picking up cues. But don't rush it. Take your beats, take your pauses, but come in sharp on the cues. That's especially true at the beginning. It's important that we get off to a fast start with this play. A lot depends on your energy to drive it forward. Now, you've got four previews. Learn how to work with the audience. By the time we open you'll have the right pace.

PATRICK: Speaking of openings, what's the word from Mecca? Is Feldman coming?

GEORGE: He'll be here for sure, Pat. We just had word today.

PHIL: Beautiful!

TOM: Yeah, I hear he's into films.

GEORGE: Don't get your hopes up. It doesn't mean the show'll go to New York. That's strictly up to Bernie.

PATRICK: God, we're such a bunch of hicks. Let a Yankee producer notice and we all sit up and wag our tails. Well, he's not going to pick all of us. We know who'll get the nod and it won't be the men.

NICK: *over the P.A.*   Forgive me, George, but can't you do that on the dinner break?

PATRICK: Which is fine by me. Besides, I'm totally against the American star system. No, really. That's why I prefer Canada. Where else can you be a top-notch actor all your life and still die broke and anonymous?

GEORGE: Okay, people, that's all for now. Are there any questions?

PATRICK: Just one. *He indicates PHIL.* Does he really have one foot longer than the other?

He starts to exit.

PHIL: I don't find that amusing.

PATRICK: I doubt if your mother does, either, sweetheart. Must cost her a fortune to keep you in footwear.

He exits.

PHIL: God, he's ridiculous. My mother hasn't bought my shoes in years.

NICK: *over the P.A.* Top of Act One in five minutes, please.

JESSICA: *rises and crosses to GEORGE* Interesting, isn't he?

GEORGE: Who?

JESSICA: Flanagan. I've never seen an actor so afraid.

GEORGE: What? Afraid Feldman won't want him?

JESSICA: No. Afraid that he will. Come along, Tommy. We've got work to do.

TOM: *as he exits with JESSICA* Jess, you know the first scene in Act Two? Does it sound funny the way I laugh? I find it hard to laugh on stage. Way harder than crying. . . .

They exit.

GEORGE stands there, thinking about JESSICA's remark. PHIL is still sitting in the armchair.

PEGGY: *rising from the table*   Phil, places have been called.

PHIL: One second, sweetheart. I want a word with George. Be right along.

PEGGY exits backstage.

GEORGE: What's the problem?

PHIL: *crosses to GEORGE*   I didn't want to bring this up in front of the others. Not around Flanagan.

GEORGE: What is it?

PHIL: I'm almost afraid to ask.

GEORGE: Don't be silly. What?

PHIL: Will there be a prompter for this show?

He peers eagerly into GEORGE's face.

GEORGE: No. From tonight on you're all on your own out there. If you get in trouble, you'll just have to rely on each other.

PHIL: George, tell me you don't mean it. Tell me it's just your gallow's humour. I can take a joke.

GEORGE: I'm sorry. We just don't have the staff. Besides, the theatre's too small. A prompter would be heard in the last row.

He starts up the aisle.

PHIL: I'll tell you what else can be heard in the last row. An actor with his mouth open and no words coming out. Is that what you want? With Bernie Feldman squirming in his seat? I ask you?

ROBERT: *to GEORGE, quickly*   I could prompt.

PHIL: God bless you.

GEORGE: *returns to the stage — to ROBERT*
I wouldn't let you within ten feet of the stage on opening night. Look what happened in *Murphy's Diamond*.

ROBERT: Anyone can faint.

GEORGE: Before the curtain goes up?

ROBERT: What do you expect? It was my first play.

GEORGE: That's right, and they weren't expecting anything. This time they'll be waiting to see the whites of your eyes.

ROBERT: Did you have to say that?

GEORGE: I just don't want you crashing onto the set in a dead swoon, so forget it. Look, Phil, you'll be great. I realize you have a problem with the odd line, but by opening night. . . .

PHIL is pacing, rubbing his stomach.

GEORGE: What's wrong?

PHIL: It's nothing, nothing.

GEORGE: Come on. What is it?

PHIL: I don't want to burden you, George. It's nothing.

He winces.

GEORGE: Phil, will you tell me what it is? Maybe I can help.

PHIL: I think it's my ulcer.

34

ROBERT: I never knew you had an ulcer.

PHIL: Neither did I. Oh, the pain, the pain. Like a kidney stone.

NICK: *over the P.A.* Should I get him a doctor?

PHIL: No, a prompter!

GEORGE: You don't need a prompter. That's all in your head. You just got off book this morning. The other actors've been off book for two weeks.

PHIL: Sure, rub it in.

GEORGE: I'm not. I'm just saying that's why you're a little unsure of the lines still. We've got four previews. By the time we open, you'll be word perfect.

PHIL: What if I dry?

GEORGE: Why should you?

PHIL: I always dry.

GEORGE: That doesn't mean you will this time. Stop thinking that way.

PHIL: George, I have long speeches in this play. Words coming out my ears. If I stumble, I could skip ten pages and not know it. You want ten minutes off the running time? I could easily slash twenty minutes off and still take all my beats and pauses.

ROBERT sits on the sofa and puts his face in his hands.

GEORGE: Phil, you worry too much. You expect to dry, so you dry. Forget the lines. I don't care if you get it word perfect. Neither does Robert. Isn't that so, Robert?

ROBERT nods, his face still in his hands.

PHIL: *not to be put off* George, take part of my salary. Pay some kid to stand in the wings with a book. I'll buy the flashlight. Only don't take away my safety net. Look at me. Knots in my stomach, it's only a preview. Think how I'll be opening night. My throat tightens. My heart, George. My heart hammers so loud in my ears I sometimes miss my first cue.

GEORGE: Calm down.

PHIL: It's so bad I once thought of taking lip-reading.

GEORGE: You're working yourself into a stew.

PHIL: I know. And to look at me you'd think I had nerves of steel, right? "Phil," they say. "Phil, you're so relaxed on stage." Oh, if they only knew, George. If they only knew inside I'm twenty different flavours of Jello and a pulse rate of one hundred and forty.

NICK: *over the P.A.* George, if Phil has recovered sufficiently I would like to get this show on the road. All actors should be in position. I would like the stage cleared.

ROBERT steps off the stage.

GEORGE: Sorry, Phil. We'll have to do this another time. Just don't underestimate yourself. You're a pro.

He takes his seat on the aisle.

PHIL: You bet your life I'm a pro. You think a novice like Tom would stand here pleading? Begging and grovelling? He hasn't had the experience. I know what it's like to be terrified: I'm a seasoned veteran. So bear that in mind when I implore you not to make me face the audience cold. Would you ask a man afraid of heights to jump from a plane without a parachute? God bless you, but there's a limit, George. A limit to what a man can do for Art. I'm only human. And don't hand me that crap you can't afford it. If you can afford to buy me shoes, you can afford a prompter.

NICK: *over the P.A.* For the last time, can we please clear the stage? We'll be starting in one minute. That's sixty seconds.

The lights begin to dim and the music starts.

PHIL: I see I'm wasting my breath. Okay, have it your way, old buddy. *He starts to exit.* Just don't say I never warned you. I love this play, and if I botch it, I'll never forgive you. *He exits backstage, only to reappear immediately.* Look, George, hear me out. I can't afford to screw up. I want Feldman to like me. Don't you see? I may never get a break like this again. That's all I'm saying.

NICK: Thirty seconds.

PHIL: You're beautiful, Nick.

And he exits.

ROBERT starts up the aisle towards GEORGE and SUSI starts down.

SUSI: *to GEORGE* Sorry, treasure, I was cleaning the lobby.

She sits in the aisle.

GEORGE: Now remember: underline anything they get wrong, no matter how small. And if Phil needs a line, give it to him.

The theatre is now dark, except for the light of the flashlight.

ROBERT: Hey, George.

GEORGE: What?

ROBERT: Why do you think they're waiting to see the whites of my eyes?

GEORGE: Robert, please! That was just a figure of speech!

Lights up on stage.

JESSICA is alone on stage, watering the hanging plants. After a moment, PATRICK comes down the stairs. He is shirtless, and is doing up his belt. He glances at JESSICA, who ignores him. He crosses to the table and pours himself a cup of coffee.

PATRICK: *with an Italian accent*   Why'd you get so upset for, Lizzie? All I asked is how long is he going to stay?

JESSICA: He's home for the holidays. That's all I know. What do you want me to do, tell him to go to a hotel? He's my son.

PATRICK: I don't like the way he looks at me. Like I'm not good enough to sit on the furniture. He'd better not start that today, because if he does, he'll wish like hell he didn't.

JESSICA: I don't want trouble, Frank.

PATRICK: *sits at the table*   Then put his nose back in joint or I'll do it for him.

The doorbell rings.

JESSICA: That's Eric, now.

She sets down the watering can and switches off the hi-fi.

PATRICK: Where the hell are my shoes?

JESSICA: Honestly, you're worse than Jimmy. *She stands behind his chair and strokes his chest.* Your shoes are upstairs. And would you please put on a shirt?

PATRICK: Lizzie, I'll give the kid two weeks. Either he's gone or I go. Make up your mind.

He rises.

JESSICA: Don't threaten me.

PATRICK: Two weeks, Lizzie.

He exits upstairs.

The doorbell rings again. JESSICA crosses into the hallway, out of sight. We hear the door open and close.

PHIL: *off* Hello, Elizabeth.

JESSICA: *off* Hi, Eric. Come in. You look half-frozen.

PHIL and JESSICA enter, PHIL taking off his overcoat. He glances into the living room. He seems quite relieved to find it empty.

JESSICA: Here. Let me take your coat. *She hangs his hat, coat, and scarf on the hatrack.* I appreciate this, Eric. I wouldn't have called if it wasn't important.

PHIL: I know that. That's why I'm here. *He crosses near the sofa.* What is it? Frank?

JESSICA: No, it's Jimmy.

PHIL: Oh?

JESSICA: Sit down. I just made a fresh pot of coffee. Have you eaten?

PHIL: Nothing for me. I had breakfast at the rectory.
. . . What's happened, Sis?

JESSICA: He's quit school.

PHIL: Jimmy quit school?

He sits on the sofa, near the arm.

JESSICA: He says he's had all he can take of university
and wants to stay here until he figures out what he wants
to do.   *She sits on the arm of the sofa.*   I don't
want him to make a mistake, Eric. I don't want him to
do something he'll regret later on.

PHIL: Well, maybe university isn't what he needs right
now.

JESSICA: *puts her hand on his*   Please, I want you
to talk to him. You're the only one who can. He won't
listen to me.

PHIL: And how's Frank feel about all this?

JESSICA: He doesn't know yet. All he knows is Jimmy's
home for the winter break.

PHIL nods. And nods. Clears his throat.

GEORGE: Patrick, that was your cue.

PATRICK: *off*   I beg to differ. My cue is Phil's line,
"I see." I didn't hear it.

PHIL: I didn't say it.

GEORGE: Did you forget?

PHIL: No, I thought I'd try not saying it. Don't you feel
the silence is more telling?

40

PATRICK: *off* The only actor I know who likes to cut his lines.

PHIL: That's because I can *act* them.

PATRICK: *off* Act all you want, mate, only don't act my cues. I'll be up here all night.

GEORGE: *to ROBERT* What do you think?

ROBERT: Cut the line. He doesn't need it.

PHIL: There. The author.

GEORGE: Okay, Patrick, take your cue from Jessica's, "Jimmy's home for the winter break." Jess, take it back to, "Let me take your coat."

PHIL: George, can I look away when she starts that crap about Jimmy? I did this time. It felt better.

GEORGE: *angrily* Look, we can't have these interruptions! We have a preview tonight! Let's just get on with it! When you're ready, Jess. Thank you.

PHIL gives GEORGE a look, then he and JESSICA get into position. He takes his overcoat off the hatrack and glances again up at GEORGE.

JESSICA: Here. Let me take your coat.

PHIL thrusts it at her.

JESSICA: I appreciate this, Eric. I wouldn't have called if it wasn't important.

PHIL: *irritably* I know that. That's why I'm here. *He crosses near the sofa.* What is it? Frank?

JESSICA: No, it's Jimmy.

PHIL: Oh?

JESSICA: Sit down. I just made a fresh pot of coffee.
     Have you eaten?

PHIL: Nothing for me. I had brunch at the rectory. . . .
     What's happened, Sis?

JESSICA: He's quit school.

PHIL: Jimmy quit school?

He sits on the sofa, near the arm.

JESSICA: He says he's had all he can take of university
     and wants to stay here until he figures out what he
     wants to do.   *She sits on the arm of the sofa.*
     I don't want him to make a mistake, Eric. I don't want
     him to do something he'll regret later on.

PHIL: Well, maybe college isn't what he needs right
     now.

He sneers up at GEORGE.

JESSICA: *puts her hand on his*   Please, I want you
     to talk to him. You're the only one who can. He won't
     listen to me.

PHIL: And how's Frank feel about all this?

JESSICA: He doesn't know yet. All he knows is Jimmy's
     home for the winter break.

PATRICK comes down the stairs, laughing.

PHIL: *rises*   Hello, Frank.

PATRICK: *to JESSICA*   You ought to see that kid of
     yours. He can't even get his socks on. What, they don't
     teach him to drink in college?   *To PHIL.*   So how's
     it going, Father? You still dipping into the poorbox?

JESSICA: Frank, you're awful.   *To PHIL.*   He's just
     pulling your leg.

PHIL: Is he?

PATRICK: Did she tell you? The kid took a swing at me
     last night.

PHIL: *puts a cigarette in his mouth*   No, Elizabeth
     never mentioned it. . . .

He fishes in his pockets for matches.

PATRICK: He thought he could drink me under the table.

He brings out his lighter and lights PHIL's cigarette.

PHIL: Thanks. . . . He's going through a very difficult
     period, Jimmy.

PATRICK: Well, he better get over it fast or he'll get
     his ass kicked.

JESSICA: Frank, please.

PATRICK: I mean it, Lizzie.

PHIL: He needs understanding right now, not brute force.

PATRICK: Is that so?

He sits on the sofa and stares at PHIL.

JESSICA: *moves behind PATRICK*   Honey, let Eric
     handle it. He knows how to talk to Jimmy. Okay?

*She leans over to kiss the top of PATRICK's head but, as
she does so, PATRICK ducks and leaps to his feet. He stares
at GEORGE, grimacing.*

GEORGE: *moving to the stage*   What's wrong?

PATRICK: I don't like that kiss. I've never liked it.
I can't do it.

GEORGE: Patrick, we can't keep starting and stopping
like this. We'll never get through the play.

PHIL: How come he doesn't get hell? I notice you don't
say he's interrupting. With him it's starting and stopping.

GEORGE: *to PATRICK*   What's wrong with the kiss?

PATRICK: I don't believe her.

JESSICA: *angrily*   Listen, you, I was doing leading
ladies when you were failing to get through adolescence.
So don't tell me how to act.

PATRICK: I forgot: she's worked with Mike Nichols.
Let's all curtsy.

JESSICA: At least I've got the guts to work outside this
country.

PATRICK: Then what the hell are you doing back here?
And don't hand me that crap about your kids needing
a mother. I don't buy it. The truth is your last two
Broadway plays died in the first week. You haven't
acted in theatre for two years. You're living in the past,
lady.

GEORGE: Okay, take it easy. Let's just solve the problem
and get back to work. We're running behind.   *To
PATRICK.*   What is it about the kiss you don't believe?

PATRICK: First of all, the priest hates my guts. He
resents the fact we're living together, and here she is
kissing me after I've just insulted him. Not only is it
unbelievable, it's maudlin.

JESSICA: It's not maudlin, it's tender. And perfectly in
character.

PATRICK: Well, it's not in character for me to let you.
At that moment Frank doesn't want to be touched.
It makes his skin crawl.

JESSICA: Well, if you think I personally enjoy it, you're
greatly mistaken. But we do make sacrifices, don't we?
Now let's get on with it.

GEORGE: Yes, we're wasting time. Maybe there's another
way to make the same point.   *He looks out at ROBERT.*
What do you think, Robert?

ROBERT: I don't see the problem. I think it works.

PATRICK: How predictable.

ROBERT: It's worked all along, hasn't it? Why does it
suddenly not work?

PATRICK: Why? Because I've never questioned it before.
I've always done it because those were the stage
directions. *Your* stage directions.

ROBERT: I see.

PATRICK: That's Phil's line. It's been cut.

ROBERT: Why're you so hostile? What did I do?

He starts down the aisle.

PATRICK: I criticize his masterpiece, and suddenly I'm
hostile.

ROBERT: That's not what I meant, and you know it.
If you've got a beef, tell me.

GEORGE: *to ROBERT*   Okay, don't get hot under
the collar.   *To PATRICK.*   Let's just cut the kiss
and get on with it.   *To JESSICA.*   Put your hand
on his shoulder. That'll make the same point.

ROBERT: *steps on stage*   No, goddamnit!

GEORGE: Look, Robert. . . .

ROBERT: *cutting in*   What the hell is this? That's a very significant and subtle moment. She's letting Eric know if it comes to a choice she'll choose Frank over him and the son. That's what the kiss means.

PATRICK: *to GEORGE*   Look, mate, get him out of here. He's done his work, now let the actors do theirs. We have enough on our hands without him on our backs.

ROBERT: I'm not on your back.

PATRICK: *in a rage*   You're here every goddamn day, aren't you? I wouldn't mind, if you cringed in a corner somewhere. But no, you pace around like a condemned man. Even when I can't see him, I can *feel* him. He's out there wringing his hands, sighing and wincing, leaping to his feet every time we drop a monosyllable, every time we change a bit of business. Christ, what's more important, George? That we observe every arbitrary stage direction or nail down a character?

GEORGE: He has a point, Robert.

PATRICK: And on top of that, he has the bloody nerve to tell me I'm incompetent.

ROBERT: I never once said that.

PATRICK: One hit play to his name, and he thinks he's hot stuff. A play that I helped create, by the way. And I've got the reviews to prove it.

ROBERT: I never said you were incompetent.

PATRICK: Maybe I've never played Washington or Dallas or New York, but I've been from one end of this country to the other.

JESSICA: So has the railroad. Get to the point.

PATRICK: *to ROBERT*   I've done it all, too, from the
     Greeks to Beckett. I even had the misfortune to be in
     two one-acters called *Lay of the Land* and *Giving
     Head*. But not even the author of those two epics had
     the audacity to walk into a theatre, as you did today,
     and say to me, "Are you getting any better?" She had
     a little more class than that.

ROBERT: So that's it.

PATRICK: And don't try to wriggle out of it.

ROBERT: That was a joke. You ought to know me better
     than that. That's just my sense of humour.

PATRICK: Sense of humour? Mate, if that's your idea of
     a joke, don't ever attempt comedy.

ROBERT: I was being ironic. I thought you knew that.

PATRICK: Try flattery next time. Irony belongs in plays.
     Irony makes me insecure. Irony makes me think you
     don't like what I'm doing.

ROBERT: Nothing could be further from the truth.
     I think you're a superb actor. One of the best actors I've
     worked with.

PATRICK: He calls that flattery. He's done two plays
     and the first had a cast of two, including myself.

JESSICA: *exasperated*   George, when you have things
     under control, let me know. I'll be in the dressing room.

She exits backstage.

PATRICK: *to ROBERT* In the future, if you have a future, don't come bouncing into rehearsal and slap an actor on the back and get cute. Just tell him he's fantastic and bite your tongue.

ROBERT: Go to hell!

NICK: *over the P.A.* George, I realize how little respect you have for stage managers, but I feel I have the right to know what's going on. Are we having a run-through or just a rehearsal? And either way, could we please carry on?

GEORGE: Oh, get off my back!

NICK: Fine. I only hope you realize that after six-thirty we'll be into overtime.

GEORGE: I could replace you with a recorded announcement.

NICK: At the rate you pay, you just might have to.

PHIL: Friends, I've been patient up to now. I've stood here and not said a word. Now I'm annoyed. No, incensed. Outraged that one member of this company is allowed to waste valuable time with his petty, childish behaviour. Not only that, he doesn't get reprimanded.

PATRICK: And who might that be, may I ask?

GEORGE: *angrily* Okay, okay, this's getting out of hand.

PHIL: *to PATRICK* If the shoe fits, old buddy. If the shoe fits.

PATRICK: Well, at least we know he's not talking about himself.

GEORGE: Goddamnit, let's stop it! *To the control booth.* Nick, let's take it from the top. As soon as you're ready.

NICK: *over the P.A.* This is a recorded announcement. Places for the top of Act One. Stand by to go in three minutes. Peggy, could you come out and pour the coffee back in the pot? And reset the chairs.

PEGGY enters and does her job.

PATRICK: *to PHIL* That was quite a speech. More than twenty words in a row and you never dried once. 'Course, it was off the cuff, wasn't it?

He smiles and exits backstage.

PHIL: *to GEORGE* Did you hear that? He wants to undermine my confidence. Well, he doesn't know it yet, but the laugh's on him. I don't have any!

He exits backstage.

GEORGE: Robert, I could've handled him, if you'd just let me. Next time, stay out of it.

ROBERT: Like hell I will. He's not pushing me around. And I'm not losing that moment.

GEORGE: Stop worrying. I'll have that moment back before we open. I promise.

ROBERT doesn't seem convinced.

GEORGE: I give you my word. Trust me.

ROBERT: George, don't say "Trust me." Anytime I hear "Trust me," I know I'm about to be screwed.

GEORGE: What're you saying? That you don't trust me? That hurts, Robert.

ROBERT: Listen, you know how long it took me to write *The Care and Treatment of Roses*. I never thought I'd even finish.

GEORGE: You had a big success with your first play. That made the second that much harder to write.

ROBERT: So what if it gets panned? What'll I have to show for three years of my life? What?

GEORGE: It won't get panned.

ROBERT: No?

GEORGE: It's a beautiful play.

ROBERT: Yeah, I know. Every play's a beautiful play. Then it gets knocked, and suddenly everyone has second thoughts. Instant hindsight.

NICK: *over the P.A.*   Two minutes to curtain.

GEORGE: I'm doing my best, okay? I want this to be bigger than *Murphy's Diamond*. Robert, this theatre's done four turkeys in a row. We need a hit or else.

ROBERT: George, they're waiting to see the whites of my eyes. I know it.

GEORGE: Forget I said that, will you?

ROBERT: No, it's true. They hate success in this country. They punish you for it. I mean, if I get slaughtered I want it to be my own fault. They don't know an actor wouldn't do a moment. He's not the one they'll blame.

GEORGE: All right, if I don't get you that moment back, I'll call every critic in town and let them know.

ROBERT: I don't want to get paranoid, George. I've seen too many people like that in this business.

NICK: *over the P.A.*   One minute to curtain. Clear the stage, please.

GEORGE: *leading ROBERT to the edge of the stage* Look, do me a favour. Go away. Go to a movie.

ROBERT: I hate movies.

GEORGE: Then get drunk.

ROBERT: I can't drink. I'm not supposed to.

GEORGE: Go home then. Take a valium and sleep until the preview.

ROBERT: I already took two libriums. That's why I'm not supposed to drink. What're you trying to say, George? You don't want me around?

GEORGE: I don't think it's wise, do you? For the sake of the play, Robert. The *play*.

ROBERT: Okay, I'll go. . . .   *He steps off the stage.* But only because you asked me, not because of Flanagan. *He starts up the aisle.*   Boy, some day I'd like to get that bastard in an alley. . . .

He smashes his right fist into his palm.

GEORGE: Robert.

ROBERT: What?

GEORGE: Take another librium, it wouldn't hurt. Or better still, work on your new play.

The stage lights are dimming and the music has begun.

ROBERT: Jesus, what a business! When you're unknown and fall on your face, they pity you. When you're successful and take a beating, they say you deserved it.

GEORGE: Forget the critics, will you?

ROBERT: Who's talking about critics? I meant my writer friends. They're far more vicious.

He exits.

GEORGE steps off the stage and takes his seat on the aisle. The theatre is now dark.

GEORGE: Stay on book, Susi, but forget what I said before. At this stage of the game, harping on lines would only demoralize them more.

Lights up on stage.

JESSICA is alone on stage, watering the hanging plants. After a moment, PATRICK comes down the stairs. He is shirtless, and is doing up his belt. He glances at JESSICA, who ignores him. He crosses to the table and pours himself a cup of coffee.

PATRICK: *with an Italian accent* Why'd you get so upset for, Lizzie? All I asked is how long is he going to stay.

JESSICA: He's home for the holidays. That's all I know. What do you want me to do, tell him to go to a hotel? He's my son.

PATRICK: I don't like the way he looks at me. Like I'm not good enough to sit on the furniture. He'd better not start that today, because if he does, he'll wish like hell he didn't.

JESSICA: I don't want trouble, Frank.

PATRICK: *sits at the table*   Then put his nose back
     in joint or I'll do it for him.

Slight pause.

JESSICA: Did you hear the doorbell?

*GEORGE leaps to his feet and glares at the control booth,
jabbing his finger in the direction of the front door.
Suddenly, there is a knocking on the door. GEORGE sits
and shakes his head.*

JESSICA: That's Eric, now.

She sets down the watering can and switches off the hi-fi.

PATRICK: Where the hell are my shoes?

JESSICA: Honestly, you're worse than Jimmy.   *She
     stands behind his chair and strokes his chest.*   Your
     shoes are upstairs. And would you please put on a shirt?

PATRICK: Lizzie, I'll give the kid two weeks. Either he's
     gone or I go. Make up your mind.

He rises.

JESSICA: Don't threaten me.

PATRICK: Two weeks, Lizzie.

He exits upstairs.

*A second knock on the door. JESSICA crosses into the
hallway, out of sight. We hear the door open and close.*

PHIL: *off*   Hello, Elizabeth.

JESSICA: *off*   Hi, Eric. Come in. You look half-
     frozen.

PHIL: *as he enters*   Not half as frozen as that doorbell.

JESSICA: Here. Let me take your coat.

NICK: *over the P.A.*   Sorry.

JESSICA: *hangs up his hat, coat, and scarf*   I appreciate this, Eric. I wouldn't have called if it wasn't important.

PHIL: I know that. That's why I'm here.   *He crosses near the sofa.*   What is it? Jimmy?

JESSICA: No, it's. . . . Yes, it is Jimmy, as a matter of fact.

PHIL: Oh.

JESSICA: Sit down. I just made a fresh pot of coffee. Have you eaten?

PHIL: Nothing for me. I just had a snack at the rectory. . . . What's happened, Sis?

JESSICA: He's quit school.

PHIL: Jimmy quit school?

He sits on the sofa, far from the arm.

JESSICA: He says he's had all he can take of university and wants to stay here until he figures out what he wants to do.   *She sits on the arm of the sofa.*   I don't want him to make a mistake, Eric. I don't want him to do something he'll regret later on.

PHIL: Well, maybe university isn't what he needs right now.

JESSICA: *in order to put her hand on his, she has to lean and stretch*   Please, I want you to talk to him. You're the only one who can. He won't listen to me.

PHIL: And how's Frank feel about all this?

JESSICA: He doesn't know yet. All he knows is Jimmy's home for the winter break.

PATRICK comes down the stairs, laughing.

PHIL: I see.

PATRICK's laughter stops, then starts again.

PHIL: *rises*   Hello, Frank.

PATRICK: I see. I see, I see, I see. . . .   *To JESSICA.* Well, you ought to see that kid of yours. He can't even get his socks on. What, they don't teach him to drink in college?   *To PHIL.*   So, Father, I see you, I see you. How's it going? You still dipping into the poorbox?

JESSICA: Frank, you're awful.   *To PHIL.*   He's just pulling your leg.

PHIL: I see!

PATRICK: Did she tell you? The kid took a swing at me last night.

PHIL: *puts a cigarette in his mouth*   No, Elizabeth never mentioned it. . . .

He fishes in his pockets for matches.

PATRICK: He thought he could drink me under the table.

He brings out his lighter to light PHIL's cigarette. PHIL bends to accept the light and, as he does so, a tall flame shoots up like a blowtorch from the adjustable lighter. PHIL recoils instinctively. He reaches for the vase of red roses on the coffee table and hurls the roses and water into

PATRICK's face. PHIL dashes around the table and, with a wild look of outrage, PATRICK starts after him. GEORGE rushes down the aisle to the stage. Pandemonium ensues.

GEORGE: Cut! Cut! Cut!

Blackout.

Music.

Act Two

The dressing room, four days later. It is 7:45 on opening night. The dressing room contains a make-up table with a mirror and four chairs, a clothes rack, and all the usual odds and ends. On the table in front of PATRICK's chair are a shoebox and an electric razor.

Downstage are two chairs separated by a small wooden stand. On the stand are a newspaper and an ashtray.

Stage right is the washroom. Upstage is the door that leads into the backstage area. Next to the dressing room, stage left, is the Green Room. It is small and contains a fridge, sofa, endtable, a telephone, and a coffee percolator on a small table. A door leads into the Green Room from the street.

Silence.

At rise, JESSICA is dressed in costume, except for her wig, which is still on the wig stand. She stands near the make-up table, buttoning her blouse. Then she crosses and looks at herself in the mirror on the washroom door.

In the Green Room, PATRICK reclines on the sofa, wearing glasses to read his script. He is dressed in a bathrobe and pants. He glances at his silver pocket watch and goes back to the script.

PEGGY enters from the street door, carrying a stack of styrofoam cups, a box of sugar cubes, and a pair of pants on a wooden hanger. She sets down the cups and the sugar, then enters the dressing room and hangs up the pants.

PATRICK: Any sign of the others?

PEGGY: Not yet, Pat.

PATRICK: What about George?

PEGGY: He still hasn't come back from dinner. I told Susi you wanted to see him.

She comes back into the Green Room and pours herself a cup of coffee.

PATRICK watches her a moment.

PATRICK: God, you're lovely. A Yeats poem made flesh. Did I try to get fresh last night?

PEGGY: Not at all.

PATRICK: I've drawn a blank, you know.

PEGGY: You were a perfect gentleman.

JESSICA: *into the mirror*   Watch him, Peg.

PATRICK: I was very fond of a girl once who looked like you.

PEGGY: I know. You told me last night.

PATRICK: I did?

PEGGY: You said I reminded you of your ex-wife.
   I thought that was very sweet.

PATRICK: What actually happened after we got back to
   my place?

PEGGY: You want the truth?

PATRICK: Not if you put it like that.

PEGGY: *entering the dressing room*   It's just that I've
   never put a man's teeth in a glass before.

PATRICK: Was it you who did that? Good God.

PEGGY: I had to. You were so drunk you might've
   choked in your sleep.

She gets the box with the actors' valuables in it.

PATRICK: Do you know how hard I searched this
   morning? I tore the house apart. For God's sake, girl,
   don't you know you never put teeth in a fridge?

JESSICA: *to PEGGY*   Darling, you just made my day.

PATRICK: Listen, you two, don't spread that around.
   You know how malicious the gossip is in this town.
   "Reputation is an idle and most false imposition; oft
   got without merit, and lost without deserving."

JESSICA: *sitting at the make-up table*   That wasn't
   from the Scottish play, I hope.

PATRICK: *Othello*. And I'm not in the least
   superstitious.

*He removes his glasses, rises and wanders into the dressing
room, aimless, restless, distracted. PEGGY smiles, blows
him a kiss, then exits into the backstage area.*

JESSICA: *after a moment*   It must be late. . . .

PATRICK: Quarter to eight.

He takes his shirt off the hanger, examines it, then takes a needle and thread from his shoebox. He sits and sews his shirt, singing a few lines from an Irish folk song.

PATRICK: Must be an easier way to make a living.

JESSICA ignores him. She is flattening out her hair with bobby pins in preparaion for the wig.

PATRICK: You know, the day I left Ireland was the day after I got married. The old man called me a lazy, shiftless sonofabitch and said I'd never do an honest day's work in my life. Imagine that.

JESSICA: How prophetic.

PATRICK: I know, and I wasn't even an actor yet. I think I became an actor just to spite him. To live out his prediction.

JESSICA turns and looks at him.

JESSICA: How do you feel?

PATRICK: Why do you ask?

JESSICA: In case you haven't noticed, you only shaved on one side of your face.

PATRICK: Did I?   *He looks in the mirror.*   So I did.

JESSICA: Your good side, naturally.

PATRICK: Instinct.   *He leans closer to the mirror.* Jesus H. Christ. . . .

JESSICA: What is it?

PATRICK: The lines around the eyes.   *Beat.*
Laugh lines. No, they are. And speaking of laugh lines,
I wish I had a few more in this friggin' play.   *He shaves.*

JESSICA: Tell me, Flanagan. Will you go to New York
if Bernie wants you? I think you'd be a fool not to.

PATRICK: *clicks off the razor*   Why wouldn't he want
me?

JESSICA: Oh, I'm sure he will. . . . The cast works so well
together. Not a single weak link. Don't you agree?

PATRICK clicks on his razor and goes back to shaving.

JESSICA: Why? Who do you think's the weak one?
Beat.   Phil?   *Beat.*   Tommy?   *Beat.*
Well, that just leaves the two of us, doesn't it?

She turns and goes back to her hair.

PATRICK: *finished shaving*   Look, don't you think
you're being a bit premature? Has Feldman read the
play?

JESSICA: And adored it. Oh, he might fault the
production, but I doubt that, it's first-rate. . . . Don't
you want to go?

PATRICK: Between you and me, I think the New York
audience is too sophisticated for this play. I think we
should leave well enough alone.

JESSICA: I never try to second guess. I only know what
I like. You thought it was good enough to do here,
didn't you?

PATRICK: New York's tougher.

JESSICA: You think so?

PATRICK: Don't you?

JESSICA: We take risks all the time, don't we? New York's just a larger arena. Higher stakes.

PATRICK: Well, I'm a Catholic and Catholics are against suicide. Besides, I don't think we should judge success by New York. No, really. I've never felt that or I'd be there, wouldn't I?

JESSICA: Flanagan, haven't you ever imagined yourself on Broadway? Let me tell you, it's the most exciting feeling in the world, bar none. And you know what's the nicest part? You feel you deserve it.

PATRICK: Yes, but how does it feel to get clobbered?

JESSICA: I wouldn't know.

PATRICK: You were in two flops.

JESSICA: The plays were; *I* wasn't.

PATRICK: Well, I'd feel I deserved it.

JESSICA: *into the mirror* Our sense of ourselves is so tentative, isn't it? I suppose that's the real risk we take.

PATRICK: What's that?

JESSICA: Facing our own failure.

PATRICK: Look, I make a damn good living here. I have my pick of roles. I might not be a star, but who is in this country? And not everyone feels that compulsion to outshine.

JESSICA: You don't need to get defensive. If you don't want to go, that's your problem. No one's twisting your arm.

PATRICK: Oh, it's a problem, is it? Christ, you sound like my ex-wife. All she ever wanted was success with a capital S. The old bitch-goddess, to quote Henry James. As if there's something wrong not wanting to work your butt off for agents and accountants and Internal Revenue.

JESSICA: Maybe she thought you were settling for too little.

PATRICK: Well, I've seen the bitch-goddess up close. I've had a sniff or two up her skirt, I know what she's like, she's insatiable, a parasite, a cancer. She gets on your back like the Old Man of the Sea and won't get off.

JESSICA: The trick is to ride success and not let it ride you.

PATRICK: Well, I'm the one who has to go out there and be good. She never understood that, my wife. She. . . . *Then, as if he has said too much already.* Look, let's drop it, shall we? And before I forget: I don't appreciate being upstaged. You did it again last night.

He enters the Green Room and pours himself a coffee.

JESSICA: When?

PATRICK: You know when.

JESSICA: I haven't the foggiest.

PATRICK: The supper scene.

JESSICA: Oh, is that why you looked so upset? I thought you had gas.

PATRICK: And while we're at it, cross your legs onstage. Last night you sat on the sofa working your legs like a pair of scissors. Freud would have a field day with that gesture.

JESSICA: I was simply working up a breeze. Didn't you find it stifling out there?

PATRICK: The first three rows don't have to know you're wearing black lace panties.

JESSICA: I bet you were the only one who noticed. Did you also notice the mark on the inside of my left thigh?

PATRICK: No, I didn't. And it was your right thigh. God knows how you got *that*. I dread to think.

JESSICA: From Mario, darling.

PATRICK: Who's Mario?

JESSICA: The little pizza boy. Don't you remember?

PATRICK: Why? Is that how you paid him?

JESSICA: No, tipped him.

Enter NICK from the street door.

NICK: Peggy, have you finished your preset? I want to open the house soon.

PEGGY: Nick, that was done ages ago.

NICK: How about Patrick? Does he have his new prop?

PATRICK: I do, and I bloody well resent the implication. *He removes a small Ronson lighter from his pocket and flicks it to produce a small, weak flame.* To cover myself I should have two of these. If they both fail, I can rub them together to get a light. *To PEGGY.* That reminds me, love. Could you please put a little more tea in the whiskey bottle? There's only one thing worse than having to drink that vile stuff and that's not having enough. Last night I had to squeeze the bottle.

JESSICA: I thought he was being cheap with his shots.

NICK: Oh, and before I forget. Jessica, you still haven't signed the callboard. Some stage managers don't mind, but I'm very, very strict about that.

JESSICA: You can see I'm here. Sign it yourself.

NICK: I'd rather you did. I don't want to start getting into bad habits. *To PEGGY.* What about the cue light? Phil was late last night on his second entrance.

PEGGY: There's nothing wrong with the cue light. He's been taking a verbal cue from Pat and he missed it.

PATRICK: He was too busy giving himself the last rites.

NICK: *to PEGGY* Well, tell him I'll cue him. I don't want that to happen again.

PEGGY: *scribbling on her clipboard* I'll remind him.

She exits into the backstage area.

NICK starts into the Green Room. He stops suddenly and turns.

NICK: *Now*, Jessica, please.

He exits out the street door.

JESSICA: Did you hear that? Who does he think he's ordering around?

PATRICK: What do you expect, reverence? I find him refreshingly democratic. He treats us all with equal contempt.

JESSICA: Well, he may be running the show now, but he better not try to give me notes. No wonder George wouldn't let him be assistant director. He has absolutely no tact.

PATRICK: I like him. He doesn't play favourites.

GEORGE enters from the backstage area. Dressed in a navy blue suit, he carries a bouquet of long-stemmed red roses and a shopping bag containing wine and presents.

GEORGE: Hello, Jess, Patrick.

JESSICA: Oh, George, am I glad to see you. Don't you look handsome.

GEORGE: *has set down the shopping bag and returned to JESSICA* You look wonderful yourself, love. *He kisses her cheek.* Radiant.

JESSICA: Hold my hand for luck. *He does.* And I thought *my* hands were cold. His are like ice. Don't be frightened, my heart. We have a wonderful play and a wonderful cast. What more could we want?

PATRICK: *entering the dressing room* A wonderful press. Knock on wood.

He taps on a downstage chair and sits, picking up a newspaper and glancing through it.

GEORGE: *hands JESSICA the flowers* These are for you, Jess. I hope you like roses.

JESSICA: I adore roses. Oh, aren't they lovely. *She stands and embraces him.* Thank you, darling.

She kisses his cheek.

PATRICK: *into his newspaper* What's in the bag, a vase?

GEORGE: Oh, God. I completely forgot.

JESSICA: That's okay. I'll find one.

GEORGE: Stay where you are. I'll get one in Props.

JESSICA: No, I insist. Besides, I have to sign the callboard or Nick'll be grinding his teeth.

She exits out the street door.

PATRICK: *to himself* Roses. How cliché!

GEORGE takes a box from the shopping bag and crosses to PATRICK.

GEORGE: For you, Pat.

PATRICK: For me? You're kidding.

GEORGE tosses him the box and PATRICK flicks off the ribbon and lifts the lid. He laughs.

GEORGE: You recognize it?

PATRICK: *removes a catcher's mask* The catcher's mask from *Murphy's Diamond*. Thanks, mate, I'm touched. No, really. That play meant a lot to me. When it closed, there was more of a hole in my life than when I got divorced. Then again, I had more fun in the play. *He puts the mask back in the box and puts the box on the stand.* Did Susi give you my message?

GEORGE: *takes two bottles of champagne from the shopping bag and crosses to the fridge* Yeah, what is it? She said it was urgent.

PATRICK: It's crucial. Did you speak to Phil about last night?

GEORGE: Yeah, I did. And believe me, he's upset enough
     already.

PATRICK: He ought to be. He botched the entire first
     act.

GEORGE: Look, it wasn't that serious. The audience
     didn't even notice.

PATRICK: How could they help but notice? There we
     are, our big scene at the breakfast table. He's right in
     the middle of his long speech, and suddenly he gets this
     strange look in his eye. "Excuse me, Frank," he says,
     and walks offstage.

GEORGE: He dried. He ran back to get his line from
     Peggy.

PATRICK: I know, and left me alone on stage. No
     dialogue, no business, nothing to do but sit there and
     eat my bacon and eggs. He was gone so long I had a
     second cup of coffee.

GEORGE: It didn't seem that long. I'm telling you, no
     one noticed.

PATRICK: George, you've never been an actor. Long
     doesn't begin to describe it. Now I know what they mean
     by a pregnant pause. By the time he came back I was in
     labour. And then he sits back down as though nothing
     has happened and says, "So as I was saying, Frank. . . ."

GEORGE: Pat, it won't happen again. Next time he'll
     just ad lib.

PATRICK: Next time?

GEORGE: If it does happen, I mean.

PATRICK: There better not be a next time, mate. Because if he walks offstage tonight, I'm walking off behind him. And I don't care if Feldman *is* in the audience.

GEORGE: Forget Feldman. I wish I'd never heard of Feldman. Chances are he won't like the show anyway.

PATRICK: That's what Jess thinks.

GEORGE: What do you mean?

PATRICK: She's heard he's not too keen on the play. That's between you and me.

GEORGE: That's ridiculous. Feldman's crazy about it. Why do you think he's coming tonight?

PATRICK: If you ask me, she's getting cold feet. Oh, she puts up a good front, but underneath she's terrified. She thinks the world will find out she's a fraud.

GEORGE: You think so?

PATRICK: I'm convinced that's why she left the States. No, really. All that crap about her kids is camouflage.

GEORGE: The thing to remember, Patrick, is that no actor has any obligation to this show after it closes here. That goes for anyone — even you.

PATRICK: Oh, I couldn't go if I wanted to. Didn't I tell you? I'm already committed to another play.

Enter JESSICA, carrying a vase.

JESSICA: No sign of Phil and Tommy? It's almost eight.

GEORGE: They may be in the theatre. I'll check with front-of-house.

JESSICA carries the vase and roses into the washroom, leaving the door ajar. She runs the water. GEORGE closes the door quickly and takes PATRICK aside.

GEORGE: *in a whisper*   What do you mean you can't do the play? That's not what you told me six weeks ago.

PATRICK: Sorry, mate, you misunderstood.

GEORGE: You knew the whole production might move to New York. I made that clear.

PATRICK: I'm sorry. I already gave my word. The director's an old, old friend of mine. I can't let him down.

GEORGE: Who is it?

PATRICK: I'm not in a position to say at the moment. Just a dear, dear friend.

GEORGE: What play are you doing?

PATRICK: What's that matter? The point is I have a commitment which I don't intend to break. I gave my word, and that's it. The subject's closed.

GEORGE: Well, the most important thing right now is that we do the play here and do it right. I don't care what happens after that.

He starts for the backstage door.

PATRICK: George.

GEORGE stops.

PATRICK: *slight pause*   I'm sorry.

GEORGE: It's okay, Pat. I understand.

PATRICK: And speak to Mastorakis again, will you? By now he's probably forgotten.

GEORGE: Relax. Stop worrying. Just go out there tonight and have fun.

He exits into the backstage area.

PATRICK: Relax, he says. That's easy for him to say. His work's done. He can sit in the dark now and chew his cuticles. I've got to go out there with a kid fresh out of theatre school and a forty-four-year-old Greek with a mind like Rip Van Winkle. Who's going to help me if *I* get in trouble?

The doorknob rattles.

JESSICA: *off*   This damn door's stuck again. Give us a pull, Flanagan.

PATRICK: One second.

He removes a bottle of whiskey from the shoebox on the make-up table and takes a long drink.

JESSICA: *off*   Flanagan!

PATRICK: Hold your horses.

NICK: *over the P.A., as PATRICK crosses to the washroom*   Good evening, ladies and gentlemen, this is your half-hour call. If you are in the theatre and have not signed the callboard, would you please do so now?

PATRICK jerks on the doorknob and the door comes flying open. JESSICA strides out.

JESSICA: If he mentions that friggin' callboard one more time, I'll ram it down his throat.

She sets the vase down on the table and begins to arrange the roses.

PATRICK begins vocal exercises with great volume and relish.

JESSICA: So who do you think's the weak one in the cast? You never said.

At that moment, SUSI enters from the backstage area with a handful of telegrams.

SUSI: Telegrams for Jessica. And Patrick. And for Tom and Phil.

PATRICK: Did you say *for* Tom and Phil? Or *from* Tom and Phil?   *He rips open a telegram and scans it.* "Best luck with *Roses*. Break your legs. Edna."

SUSI: Shouldn't that be "break a leg"?

PATRICK: Not if you knew my ex-wife. She's very precise.

SUSI: I didn't know you were married, Patrick.

PATRICK: Neither did I, love. That's why she divorced me.

JESSICA: This one's from Innerkip. "Knock 'em dead." Signed. "Percy."

PATRICK: Who's Percy?

JESSICA: I haven't the foggiest. Where the hell is Innerkip?

PATRICK: Never mind Innerkip. Where the hell is Tom and Phil?

GEORGE enters from the backstage area.

GEORGE: Susi, Nick's looking for you. He wants to open the house.

SUSI: He's gotta be kidding. It's like a greenhouse in there.

GEORGE: Speak to him. That's between the two of you. . . . Can I see you a moment, love? The Green Room. . . . *To PATRICK and JESSICA.*   I'll be right back.

He guides SUSI into the Green Room. PATRICK and JESSICA continue to read their telegrams.

SUSI: I know. Keep my voice down.

GEORGE: I don't want them to know I'm worried. Nick's trying to locate the others. Did Tom say what he was doing today?

SUSI: How should I know?

GEORGE: I thought he was at your place last night.

SUSI: George, give me a break. I know Phil was shooting a film this afternoon. Some industrial film.

GEORGE: Where?

SUSI: He didn't say.

GEORGE: Would his girlfriend know?

SUSI: Gloria? She might. His mother'd know for sure. He has to call in once a day or she phones Missing Persons.

GEORGE: You have her number?

SUSI: She's in the lobby.

GEORGE: Great. Ask her where he's working and have
    Nick call them.

SUSI: Right.   *She starts out, then turns.*   What about
    Feldman? Should I bring him back as soon as he picks
    up his tickets?

GEORGE: No, keep him out. I don't want him around
    Patrick. Where's Robert?

He sits on the sofa.

SUSI: Upstairs in the shop.

GEORGE: What's he doing up there?

SUSI: Shaving.

GEORGE: Well, tell him to get his ass down here on
    the double. Give him a bottle of champagne from the
    office. Tell him it's for the cast.

SUSI: Will do.

She exits.

*In a rage GEORGE hammers his fists on the sofa and stamps
his feet. PATRICK and JESSICA exchange a glance.*

GEORGE: *to himself*   Jesus Christ, tonight of all
    nights. . . .

*He takes a cigarette from a pack on the endtable, lights it,
removes his wristwatch and glances at the time. Composing
himself, he enters the dressing room.*

GEORGE: *with a hearty, but false expansiveness*   Well!

PATRICK: *suspiciously*   Worried, are you?

GEORGE: What makes you think I'm worried?

PATRICK: One: you're chewing the inside of your cheek. Two: you're carrying your wristwatch.

JESSICA: And three: you're smoking the filter.

Enter PHIL from the street door. He is out of breath and visibly upset. He wears sunglasses and a beret. Under his arm is a much-worn copy of the script.

PHIL: Forgive me, people. I apologize. It's inexcusable. George, old buddy, don't look at me like that. I'm not to blame. I swear to God.

He puts down his script and kicks off his shoes.

GEORGE: Where've you been?

PHIL: *crosses to the clothes rack and removes his shirt* They ran overtime. They knew I had an opening tonight, and they still lied about the time. I will never buy my mother another Singer sewing machine.

JESSICA: Did you sign the callboard? You better or Hitler will chew you out.

PHIL: Hitler?

JESSICA: Our stage manager.

PHIL: I signed already. Oh, George, do you know if Gloria's picked up her ticket?

GEORGE: She's in the audience.

PHIL: I wasn't sure she'd come.

JESSICA: Don't tell me you two are still fighting?

PHIL: Can you blame us? Every time we discuss marriage my mother goes to bed and refuses to eat.

He removes his pants. He's wearing a pair of bright red bikini briefs.

PATRICK: Well, look at *her*. Red bikinis. Very, very smart, love. A gift from mother? Or a pair of mother's?

PHIL: *putting on the priest's pants*   I always wear red opening night. I feel like a bullfighter. It's gore or be gored.

JESSICA: *to PATRICK*   Don't you make fun of Phil. At least he doesn't bring his make-up in a shoebox.

PHIL sits down at the table and opens a fishing tackle box and removes his pancake make-up.

PHIL: That's right. You're a disgrace to the profession.

PATRICK: I never wear make-up. Haven't you noticed? I like to be the first out.

PHIL: Then what's in the shoebox?

PATRICK: My laundry. I always do it every two weeks.

PHIL removes his sunglasses. He leans forward to examine his left eye in the mirror. JESSICA glances his way, does a double take, then stares.

JESSICA: Oh, my God, he's got a black eye. Look.

PHIL: It's nothing, nothing.

GEORGE: Let me see.   *He inspects the eye.*   Phil, how did you do that?

PHIL: I can't tell you. I'm too ashamed. Please, I'm okay. Don't be alarmed.

JESSICA: *crosses into the Green Room to the fridge*   I'll get some ice.

PATRICK: He calls me a disgrace, and he shows up
tonight with a black eye.

GEORGE: Forget the ice, Jess. There isn't time. Phil,
you'll have to hide it with make-up. How's your vision?

PHIL: *as JESSICA returns*   Twenty-twenty, old buddy.
I just can't feel my cheekbone. But compared to my
hand, George. My hand.

GEORGE: What's wrong with your hand?

PATRICK: He's been hitting himself again. I told you to
stop doing that.

PHIL: Just what I'd expect from you. I'm in exquisite
pain, and he laughs.

GEORGE: Let's see.

PHIL holds out the hand.

GEORGE: Looks fine to me.

PHIL: I think it's broken. The index finger. Look: blue.
A hairline fracture, at least. Oh, God, God. Why tonight?

He continues getting dressed.

GEORGE: So what happened?

PHIL: Incredible, huh? I can't believe it. Phil Mastorakis.
I hate violence with a passion. I'm squeamish. That dumb
film. That's what did it. Take after take after take. And
to lie to me, to deceive me about the time. A rage,
George. I was in a rage when I left. Stormed out. Two
blocks later it happened.

GEORGE: What happened?

PHIL: The fight. The fistfight. How do you think I got this shiner?

GEORGE: *exasperated*   Phil, that's what I'm trying to find out!

PHIL: These two musclemen, right? They're strolling towards me. I.Q. tattooed on their biceps. With a penknife. I go to pass, one turns to the other and says, "Artiste!" I went berserk, George. I saw red. I ran back and took a swing at the guy. Next thing I know I'm sitting on the sidewalk, my beret in my lap, some guy walks by and drops in a quarter.

He tosses his beret on the make-up table.

GEORGE: That was a crazy thing to do, Phil. You could've been killed.

PHIL: I know, I know, don't remind me. And you know what's even crazier? For twenty years I've wanted to be called an artist in this country, and the first guy who says it I punch him.

Enter NICK and PEGGY from the street door.

NICK: George, the house is in. I've been calling — Oh, hello, Phil, you're here.   *To GEORGE.*   Thanks for letting me know.

JESSICA: Obviously, you never checked the callboard. *To PHIL.*   Did I tell you? Nick is very, very strict about that.

NICK: All kidding aside, I haven't been able to reach Tom. Does anyone know where he went today?

PHIL: *shocked*   He's late?

NICK: Take it easy, Phil. I'm sure there's no need to panic.

PHIL: Fine. Great. Fantastic. We go up in twenty minutes, and there's no need to panic?

GEORGE: Nick's right. Maybe he got held up in traffic. *To NICK.* Did you call his new number?

NICK: Naturally I called his new number, George. There was no answer. If I'd called his new number and spoken to him, I wouldn't be here now asking the cast if anyone knew where he was, would I?

GEORGE: Listen, you pompous ass. . . .

PHIL: *cutting in* I think he mentioned a wedding. Yeah, he did. He had a wedding to go to.

JESSICA: A wedding?

PHIL: His father was getting married again. That's why he couldn't make the opening.

NICK: What church? Do you know?

PHIL: Wasn't in a church. He was getting married in his backyard. Weather permitting.

NICK: Do you know where he lives?

PHIL: Let's see. I wasn't paying that much attention. . . . No, I'm sorry. I can't . . . I can't. . . .

He shrugs.

PATRICK: The word is remember.

PHIL: Hey, look, Flanagan . . .

GEORGE: *cutting in* Phil, it might help if we know his first name. Did Tom ever mention it?

PHIL: His first name, huh? Let's see. I'm lousy with names. God. it's right on the tip of my tongue.

GEORGE: Think hard.

PHIL: Okay, but don't stand over me like that. I have to do this my way.... Tom and I had lunch at Luigi's on Tuesday. He ordered french fries and a cheeseburger with the works ...

GEORGE: *cutting in* I don't care what he ate, just his father's name.

PHIL: I'm working up to it.... And I ordered an egg salad sandwich on brown and a chocolate milkshake. No, a *toasted* egg salad sandwich on brown.

PATRICK: I hope they didn't have dessert.

PHIL: We'd just got our order and Tom said he had to go to a wedding the afternoon of the opening.

GEORGE: What did you say?

PHIL: I asked who was getting married.

GEORGE: And he said?

PHIL: His old man.

GEORGE: *exasperated* Phil, we know that!

PHIL: Only he didn't say his old man. They call each other by their first names. How often do you hear a father and son ... ?

GEORGE: *cutting in — he grabs PHIL by the front of his shirt* The name, Phil! Just the name!

PHIL: Percy.

JESSICA: Percy? Oh, my God, Tommy's in Innerkip.

GEORGE: Innerkip?

JESSICA: See for yourself.   *She hands him the telegram.*   It must be his. There must've been a mix-up.

GEORGE: *as he reads*   Where's Innerkip?

JESSICA: Listen, until a second ago we never knew who Percy was.

NICK: *to GEORGE, taking the telegram*   I'll get on it right away.

He enters the Green Room and uses the phone, quietly ad libbing his phone calls.

PEGGY, who has been sitting on the sofa, rises and wanders into the dressing room. She and GEORGE exchange a worried glance.

JESSICA: What time is it?

PEGGY: Exactly 8:12.

JESSICA: 8:12. Almost time for, "Ladies and gentlemen, this is your fifteen minute call." So help me, if his voice comes over that box, I'll kill him.

NICK overhears this remark and makes an obscene gesture.

JESSICA: *puts on her wig and turns to GEORGE*
There. How do I look? Don't tell me: ghastly. Cheap and ghastly.

GEORGE: You look gorgeous. It's perfect.

JESSICA: Liar. It's horrid and you know it. I look like a Barbi doll for octogenarians.

She returns to the mirror and begins to comb her wig.

ROBERT enters from the street door, carrying a bottle of champagne. There are bits of kleenex stuck to his chin, cheek and neck from where he has cut himself shaving.

PATRICK: Oh-oh, just what we needed: Banquo's ghost.   *To JESSICA, quickly.*   And I didn't quote the Scottish play.

JESSICA: No, but you came bloody close. Hello, Robert. Pull up a chair. I take it you've heard?

ROBERT: Heard what?

JESSICA: About Tommy.

ROBERT: I heard he was late, that's all.

JESSICA: That's all I meant, darling.

ROBERT sits in the chair downstage left, clutching the bottle.

JESSICA: Peg, be a dear and take that bottle. If he holds it any tighter, he'll pop the cork.

PEGGY tries to take the bottle. ROBERT clutches it even tighter.

ROBERT: That's for the cast. Right, George?

GEORGE nods and looks away. ROBERT lets PEGGY take the bottle.

PEGGY: I'll put it in the fridge.

She does, and sits on the sofa in the Green Room.

JESSICA: *crosses and sits in the other downstage chair*
Chin up, darling. This is your big night. Did I tell you?
Bernie called from New York. He wants to meet you
after the show.

ROBERT: Jess, I'm not going on, I'm not an actor. I
don't know the blocking, I don't even know the lines.
Besides, I don't look the part, and I'm too old. And on
top of that I think I got the flu, I don't feel so hot.

GEORGE: Robert, if it came to that, I'd go on with the
script. Now why don't you take a walk? The air would
do you good.

JESSICA: Have you eaten today?

ROBERT: I'm not hungry.

PHIL: I bet he never slept much, either. Huh, Flanagan?

PATRICK: What's that mean?

ROBERT: I never slept a wink. My girl said I was driving
her nuts. My teeth were chattering.

JESSICA: Was it cold last night?

ROBERT: Hot.

JESSICA: Oh.

ROBERT: She said my feet were cold, too. My hands.
My nose. My . . .

PATRICK: *cutting in* Spare me the rest, mate. I live
alone. I have my own problems with women.

GEORGE: Maybe you ought to lie down, Robert. I'll
let you know the moment Tom arrives.

JESSICA: *to ROBERT* Don't fret, my heart. I worry about shows that go too smoothly. I was in four Broadway shows and each one barely made it to curtain.

PATRICK: I beg to differ. I happened to star in his first play and the only crisis we had was the one he wrote in the second act.

PHIL: That's not what I heard.

PATRICK: Then again, he has a right to fret. His first work was called a play. This one's being touted as a vehicle. A vehicle for Miss Jessica Logan. From Art to Mechanics at one fell swoop.

JESSICA: *springs to her feet* All right, you sonofabitch, *that* was from *Macbeth*.

PATRICK: What? "One fell swoop?"

JESSICA: If you have no respect for yourself at least have some for tradition. Right now we need all the luck we can get. Or don't you want this show to go on?

She returns to the make-up table. PATRICK takes her chair.

PATRICK: Look, how can we miss? We have a star in the cast, Robert. Not like *Murphy's Diamond*. We have a real star. A star that can lure Bernie Feldman up to the boondocks.

JESSICA: It also helps if the play is good.

PATRICK: *to JESSICA* By the way, I loved your interview in the *Globe*. *He holds up the newspaper.* Isn't it noble of Miss Logan to act in a new play at a two hundred seat theatre? No dressing room of her own. No star on the door. Working for scale with local character actors.

PHIL: Hey, get off her back, why don't you?

PATRICK: That's from the play, isn't it? Are you talking to me or just running lines?

PHIL: I've had it up to here with you and your sick jokes. This is a real lady here, and that's more than I can say for you.

JESSICA: Why don't you save your nastiness for Act One and just let the rest of us get into character?

PATRICK: Don't pull rank on me.

JESSICA: I'm not pulling rank. I'm simply telling you to shut your mouth. Is that clear? I don't want to hear about Bernie Feldman or being a star or anything else you care to dredge up to cover your own fear.

PATRICK: *My* fear?

JESSICA: And as for New York, Buster, I wouldn't want you in the cast anyway. After this show closes here, I'll be quite happy to read your obituary, you black Irish bastard.

ROBERT: Jess, I feel weird. I'm dizzy. My ears are ringing. . . .

JESSICA: *crosses to ROBERT* Quick. Put your head between your knees.

He does.

JESSICA: Don't move. Phil, where're your smelling salts?

PHIL: *darts to the make-up table and back* Here.

JESSICA: Sit up, Robert.

He does.

JESSICA: Now breathe in. *She puts the bottle under his nose.* That's it. Again.

NICK hangs up the phone.

NICK: What's wrong with him?

JESSICA: What does it look like?

ROBERT: Jess. . . .

JESSICA: What, my heart?

ROBERT: I think I'm going to be sick. . . .

He bolts up, covers his mouth, and lurches out the street door.

PATRICK: What was wrong with the washroom? Be just our luck if he brings up all over a critic.

He enters the washroom, closing the door.

PHIL: Get them first. That's what I always say.

NICK: *to GEORGE*   Why'd you let him back here? You ought to know better than that.

GEORGE: Did you have any luck with Tom? Did you reach his father?

NICK: There was no answer. I called the local police. They said they'd send a car to the house. At least we'll know if he's still there.

GEORGE: Good thinking.

NICK: All we can do now is wait.   *He starts out the street door, then turns back to GEORGE.* I don't mind you being back here, but *don't* upset the actors.

He exits.

JESSICA: There. He did it again.

GEORGE: Fascist!

JESSICA: Why do you stand for it? Why don't you send him packing?

GEORGE: Are you kidding? He's the best stage manager we ever had.

Pause. PEGGY stretches out on the sofa as though she has a headache.

PHIL: Anyone have a cigarette?

GEORGE: I thought you quit.

PHIL: *as JESSICA passes him a cigarette*   Seven years ago, but now and then I get the urge. Right now I need a cigarette.

He lights up.

GEORGE: By the way, how are the new shoes? Do they fit?

PHIL: Perfectly.

GEORGE: I'm glad to hear it.

Pause. PHIL puffs on his cigarette.

PHIL: Except they squeak. They're brand new, George. I liked that second pair better. Too bad they were tight in the arches.

Pause. He puffs again.

PHIL: I have a high arch.

GEORGE: Yes, I know.

Pause.

JESSICA: Is that what that was, your shoes? I thought we had a loose floorboard.

GEORGE: You could hear it?

JESSICA: Hear it? I expected to fall through the set. Where were you sitting?

GEORGE: The last row. I never heard a thing.   *He crosses to the imaginary doorway of the Green Room.* Peggy, can't we get him a pair of shoes that don't squeak?

PEGGY: *immobile on the sofa, her eyes closed*   Not for tonight we can't.

GEORGE: Well, can't we oil them?

PEGGY: George, you don't oil shoes, you oil a hinge. Shoes you wear in.

Just then, TOM rushes into the Green Room. He looks desperate. He is dressed in a suit and tie; the tie loose, the jacket in his hand.

TOM: Oh, Jeez, I'm sorry, I'm sorry. Honest. I'm sorry, everybody. Don't be mad.

JESSICA: Oh, thank God.

TOM: I know: I'm late. I'll get dressed.

He crosses to the clothes rack and begins to tear off his clothes.

GEORGE: Slow down, Tom. Don't get yourself all worked up.

TOM: My first part, and this happens. I can't think straight. It's like a nightmare.

He rips off his shirt, popping the buttons.

PEGGY puts on her headset which is on the wall in the Green Room.

PEGGY: Nick, Tom's here. He just arrived.

TOM: A goddamn nightmare.

PEGGY: Yeah, he'll be dressed in a flash.

GEORGE: What kept you, Tom?

TOM: *removing his pants*   My dad got married. He would've been hurt I hadn't gone. Like, I didn't want to go. It's eighty miles outside the city. I hate that place.

GEORGE: Innerkip?

TOM: How'd you know?

GEORGE: Tell you later.

TOM: *puts on his pajama top*   I left plenty of time to make it back. 'Cept the cab had a flat. I never knew cabs got flats. I thought they weren't like other cars. Isn't that crazy?

GEORGE: How long's it take to fix a flat? A few minutes?

TOM: Sure, if you got a spare. Like, he had no spare. Can you believe it? No spare. I mean, there we are trying to flag down another cab on the highway. Jeez, you can never get a cab when you want one. Oh yeah, I forgot. Someone. . . . Like, could someone play the driver? I'm a little fixed for cash.

PHIL: Play the driver?

JESSICA: Fixed for cash?

PEGGY: I'll take care of it.

GEORGE: Peggy, tell Nick to get down right away. On the double.

PEGGY exits. GEORGE enters the Green Room and bites his hand.

TOM: Jeez, what a driver, Phil. I mean, his right arm, like it's in an elbow cast.   *He giggles.*   He's really something. We're driving along, his good arm's out the window, he's singing *Rigoletto* and closing his eyes on the high notes. Oh, Phil, he knows you. He thinks you're the greatest.

PHIL: *pleased*   Oh, yeah?

The toilet flushes and PATRICK has to use force to get the washroom door open. He stands staring at TOM. GEORGE enters from the Green Room. TOM notices everyone watching him.

TOM: Well, he *said* it was *Rigoletto*.

JESSICA: He's drunk. Oh, my God, Tommy's *pissed*.

GEORGE: I know, I know.

PATRICK: Jesus H. Christ.

He turns away in disgust. PHIL puts his face in his hands.

TOM: No, really, I'm fine. Honest. Look: I'm fine.

GEORGE: What'd you have to drink, Tom?

TOM: Just punch.

PHIL: Punch?

TOM: Pineapple punch.

GEORGE: What was in it?

JESSICA: Need you ask? Look at him. He can't even focus.

GEORGE: Tell me the truth, Tom. How drunk are you? Can you go on?

TOM: Better believe it.

He is struggling to get his pajama bottoms on over his slippers.

GEORGE: *taking PATRICK aside*   We have to risk it, Pat. What choice do we have?

PATRICK: In that condition? I'm not going on stage with young Barrymore till he's dead sober. George, it's hot out there. He'll fall asleep on the sofa. Stick his head in the sink.

He rushes into the Green Room and pours a coffee. PHIL puts on his scarf and overcoat.

JESSICA: *helping TOM on with his pajama bottoms*   Here we go. One leg at a time. That's it.

TOM: *to JESSICA*   Know what my dad thinks? He thinks I got drunk because I hate the bitch he married. That wasn't the reason. I just didn't know the spike was punched.

JESSICA: *to GEORGE*   And he has to make it through a four page monologue.

She returns to the make-up table.

TOM: Jesus H. Christ.

PATRICK: *returns with the coffee*   That's my line, mate, get your own. Here, drink this. Faster, faster. There's another gallon where that came from. Okay, George, he's all yours. Just don't drown him.

GEORGE: Come on, Tom.

He leads TOM into the washroom, leaving the door slightly ajar.

PATRICK: And just remember, Thomas, my lad, no matter how much you may want to go to the can, don't walk offstage before intermission. I already had one actor pull that.

PHIL: Then don't cross your eyes in the middle of my speech. That's why I dried.

PATRICK: I never crossed my eyes.

PHIL: No? What would you call it?

PATRICK: Maybe I winced a little.

PHIL: Winced?

PATRICK: And no bloody wonder. Lay off those Greek salads. There was enough garlic on your breath to shrivel the balls on a brass monkey. How's he doing, George? Is he sober and repentant?

PHIL: Don't hand me that. You accused me of walking offstage just to spite you. And in the vilest, filthiest gutter language.

PATRICK: You dreamt it.

PHIL: I suppose my mother dreamt it, too? She was sleeping on the couch. She heard every word.

GEORGE and TOM come out of the washroom, TOM drying his head with a towel. He squirts water from between his teeth and grins.

PATRICK: I wish I found that amusing.

Enter NICK.

NICK: How is he? Can he go on?

GEORGE: I need time to sober him up. Make an announcement. Tell the audience there's been a delay, we may go up late. I'll walk him around the block.

NICK: We can't hold much past 8:45. Nine at the latest.

GEORGE: Listen, we'll hold as long as it takes. We're not cancelling the show unless the actors want to. Is that understood?

NICK: Perfectly.

GEORGE: If I can just get him to the point where he can say, "The punch is spiked."

TOM: *looks up*   I don't say that, do I?

GEORGE: Let's go, Tom. Let's take a walk. Better still, let's jog. On your mark. Go.

He starts off with TOM trailing behind, the towel draped around his neck. They exit.

PATRICK: If Robert thinks he's sick now, wait'll he sees George and Tom jogging around the block.

He sits at the make-up table.

PHIL: Nick, what's it like out there?

JESSICA: Like a greenhouse, according to Susi.

PHIL: That's the last time. I'll never do another show in May. Not in a theatre without air-conditioning.

NICK: We do have a fan.

PHIL: The critics'll hate our guts. They'll be stuck to the chairs.

JESSICA: *to NICK* Did you sign Tommy in? I wouldn't want you suddenly remembering your precious callboard right in the middle of a sound cue.

PATRICK: Look, why don't you ease up? He's only doing his job.

NICK: That's okay, Pat. I've been through enough openings to know Jessica's not really mad at me.

He smiles and exits.

JESSICA: I wouldn't let him direct latecomers to their seats, let alone a play.

PHIL: I can see it now: two hundred people, wilting, their glasses steaming. Sneaking cold apple cider into the theatre. What a thought. Two hundred crunching plastic cups. Imagine what that'll do to our silent moments?

He stands and begins to limber up.

JESSICA: What time is it?

PHIL: Five minutes to curtain.

JESSICA: This's what happens when you don't have understudies.

PHIL: Understudies? They're too cheap to hire a prompter.

Suddenly he reacts, turns and sits at the make-up table.
He takes his script and runs lines.

Pause.

JESSICA: I wonder why Bernie hasn't come back. That's
   not like him.

Slight pause.

JESSICA: If there's anything I loathe, it's waiting.

PHIL: We could run lines. . . .

PATRICK and JESSICA greet this remark with incredulous
looks.

PHIL: Just a thought. . . .

NICK: *over the P.A.*   Ladies and gentlemen, may I
   have your attention, please. Due to technical difficulties,
   the curtain will go up a few minutes late. We're working
   on it, so please bear with us. Thank you.

Pause.

PHIL: Nights like this I wish I'd never heard of John
   Garfield.

JESSICA: John Garfield?

PHIL: Did you ever see *Gentlemen's Agreement*? He
   was wonderful. I walked out that day wanting to be an
   actor. He make it look so easy.

Pause.

PATRICK: The intangibility of the stage. A few remembered moments that add up to a life. *Beat.* Like pissing into the wind. *Slight pause.* I can't remember why I became an actor. Not that it matters. *Beat.* No, that's not true. I do remember: to get laid.

PHIL: God, if that isn't pathetic.

PATRICK: It is, but I get laid a lot.

Enter PEGGY from the street door.

PEGGY: Jesus, Mary, and Joseph. Even that cab driver wants to be in show business. I could've killed him. He pulled me into his cab, Pat, and you wouldn't believe what he did.

PATRICK: *Rigoletto.*

PEGGY: How'd you know that?

JESSICA: *hands PEGGY her brush* Peggy, would you mind? See if you can't comb out some of the cheapness. I think they stole it from Woolworth's.

PATRICK: *picks up the shoebox* The trouble with this company is there's no juicy young ingénue to corrupt.

PHIL: You're contemptible. No wonder you live alone.

PATRICK: I don't give a fiddler's damn what you think, Father. Amen, Patrick. Say three Hail Marys and put four cents in the poorbox.

He starts for the washroom.

JESSICA: Where do you think you're going?

PATRICK: *stops* To the WC, teacher. Did I forget to raise my hand?

JESSICA: Stop him, Phil. He's got a bottle.

PHIL: A bottle?   *He bounds from his chair and gets between PATRICK and the washroom.*   Okay, old buddy, I'll take that. Hand it over.

He snaps his fingers.

PATRICK: Do that again, I'll break your arm. Now get out of my way.

PHIL: Did you hear that? He threatened me.

JESSICA: What the hell do you think you're doing, drinking before an opening? Where's George? I won't step on that stage tonight if this sonofabitch takes a drink.

Enter GEORGE and TOM, both gasping for breath. GEORGE now has the towel draped around <u>his</u> neck. TOM appears to have sobered considerably. He halts at the coffee percolator and pours himself a black coffee.

GEORGE: Peggy, what time is it?

PEGGY: 8:31.

PATRICK replaces the shoebox on the make-up table. GEORGE puts on PEGGY's headset.

GEORGE: Nick, are you in the booth? . . . Okay, we can go anytime you're ready. Tom's much better. . . . Yeah, he'll be fine. He doesn't go on until five minutes into the first act.

He replaces the headset.

TOM exiles himself in the Green Room and stares at the floor.

NICK: *over the P.A.* Okay, cast, we'll be starting in exactly five minutes. So stand by beginners for Act One. Have a good show.

PATRICK, JESSICA and PHIL each sit and give last minute attention to themselves in the mirror. GEORGE crosses to JESSICA.

GEORGE: *kisses her cheek* Good show, love. I'll see you later.

JESSICA: Are you watching the show?

GEORGE: No, I'll be in the lobby.

JESSICA: Would you have your wife sit near the front?

GEORGE: Why?

JESSICA: I want to know if she can see up my skirt. Tell her to sneeze once for yes.

GEORGE crosses to PATRICK who is running a lint brush over his pants.

GEORGE: What can I say, Pat?

PATRICK: A simple "Thank you" would suffice. "You're a helluva great actor" would be even better.

GEORGE: How about both?

PATRICK: Terrific, mate. Only next time think of it yourself.

GEORGE moves to PHIL.

GEORGE: Phil.

PHIL: *staring into the mirror* Oh, gentle Jesus, my eye, George. My eye's closing. See.

GEORGE: We'll have it looked after at intermission. I have to go, Phil.

PHIL: How do I explain this to my mother?

GEORGE: Phil, listen. Just tell me one thing: can you go on? That's all I need to know.

PHIL: *leaps to his feet* Oh, God, George, if that isn't pathetic. You have to ask Phil Mastorakis whether or not he can go on. And you want to know what's even more pathetic? I don't think I can!

PATRICK crosses to TOM.

PATRICK: Hey, what the hell you doing? This's your baptism here tonight. Hold up your head, you're an actor.

TOM does.

PATRICK: It's not the end of the world. I don't hold it against you. Neither do the others. You know what happened to me my first opening?

TOM: What?

PATRICK: Nothing. It went like clockwork. I got a rave review.

TOM: *grins* Shit.

PATRICK: I almost did. I didn't believe a word of it. Here. *He reaches into his pocket and brings out his pocket watch.* Take this.

TOM: I can't take your watch.

PATRICK: I want you to have it. *He drops the watch into TOM's hand.* Think of it as a baptism present. My old man gave that to me as a talisman the day I went into show business. He was so proud, the old bugger.

TOM: Thanks, Pat.

PATRICK: *lifting TOM to his feet*   Besides, Tom, it
could've been worse. You could've dropped dead jogging
round the block. Then where would we be? George
would have to walk through the part. Or Robert, perish
the thought.

He nudges TOM into the other room.

TOM: *to GEORGE, showing him the watch*   My dad
didn't give me anything.

GEORGE: Have a good show, Tom. Everyone.

*As the actors prepare to go on, GEORGE crosses into the
Green Room to exit but is met by SUSI coming in.
She puts her finger to her lips.*

GEORGE: Don't tell me. If it's bad news, I don't want
to hear.

SUSI: The babysitter just called. Your wife's in the
hospital. She tripped on the way down the steps and
broke her leg.

GEORGE: *leans against the door*   Oh, God, I thought
you were going to tell me Feldman couldn't make it.

SUSI: You never let me finish. He just called from the
airport. His plane was late getting in. Soonest he could
be here, he said, was forty minutes.

GEORGE: We can't hold the curtain that long. I don't
care who he is.   *Beat.*   Can't he get here any
faster?

SUSI: He's just as upset as you are.

GEORGE: Well, he'll have to see the show tomorrow.
He can't judge the show on the last act.

SUSI: Tomorrow's fine with him. He sounded very nice.

GEORGE: The actors won't like it. The second night is always a letdown.

The actors, aware that something is going on in the Green Room, are all staring in that direction.

SUSI: Should I tell them? I don't mind doing your dirty work.

GEORGE: Don't you dare or we'll have the letdown tonight. I wouldn't mind telling Patrick, only he'd never keep his mouth. . . .

He puts a finger to his lips and crosses to the imaginary doorway between the two rooms. All four actors are staring at him.

GEORGE: Good show, everyone.

He raises his arm in a salute. Slowly all four actors raise an arm, almost in perfect unison.

GEORGE: *to SUSI, as they exit*   What hospital's she in? . . .

NICK: *over the P.A.*   Peggy, are beginners in place? It's two minutes to curtain.

JESSICA: Two minutes? Oh, my God, what am I doing here? I could be home, knitting.

PEGGY: *into her headset*   No, they're not, Nick. Not quite.

NICK: *over the P.A.*   Actors, places have been called.

PEGGY gets her flashlight and crosses to the door that leads into the backstage area. She holds open the door and waits.

JESSICA: I could crochet a better wig than this.

PATRICK: Peggy, did someone turn the fan off? I'm not shouting above that racket.

JESSICA: I think brushing only brought out the shine.

PHIL: *putting on his shoes* A pair of shoes that don't squeak. Is that a lot to ask?

PATRICK: *flicking his lighter repeatedly* I ought to tell George to stick this. What's he think I'll do, burn down the theatre? I'm bloody well insulted.

JESSICA: I could've bought a wig. Or borrowed one. Why didn't I? *To PEGGY, plaintively.* Oh, Peggy. . . .

PHIL: *pacing* With these shoes, they'll hear us going on in the dark.

JESSICA: With this on my head, they'll probably *see* us.

By now, all three actors are lined up at the door. PEGGY flicks on her flashlight and exits. TOM is seated at the make-up table, applying make-up between sips of coffee.

JESSICA: *about to exit* I don't know why she needs a flashlight. I give off enough light for all of us.

She pats her wig and exits.

PATRICK: *shouts out the door* Spoken like a true star.

JESSICA: *pokes her head back in* Bet your ass.

She exits.

PATRICK: *to PHIL* Listen, mate, would it throw you too much if I use matches instead?

He wheels and exits.

PHIL: *to TOM*   He doesn't even wait for an answer.

He notices the shoebox. He snatches it up and rushes into the washroom, leaving the door open.

TOM: Phil, what're you doing?

PHIL: *off*   Dumping his laundry down the sink. This'll teach him a good lesson.

TOM closes the door so as to be able to inspect himself in the full-length mirror.

NICK: *over the P.A.*   Okay, here we go. Have a good show, everyone. Stand by. House to half. Light cues one through four. Preshow out and sound cue one.

The doorknob rattles.

PHIL: *off*   Tom! Tom!

TOM: What?

PHIL: *off*   I'm locked in! Oh, Jesus, Jesus, Sweet Saviour, I'm locked in!   *He kicks and pounds on the door.*   Get me out! Get me out!

TOM rushes over and struggles to pull open the door. PEGGY darts back into the room.

PEGGY: What's going on? Where's Phil?

TOM: In the can. . . .

At that moment, the doorknob comes off in his hand and he goes backwards head over heels and knocks himself out. PEGGY rushes to TOM, sees that he's unconscious, and grabs her headset.

PEGGY: John, don't go on light cue one. Nick, Phil's locked in the washroom and Tom's out cold. Better send someone right down. . . . Okay, I'll tell them we're holding.   *She crosses to the washroom.*   Phil, don't panic. We'll have you out of there in a minute. Phil, did you hear what I said?

PHIL: *off*   I'm too moved to speak.

PEGGY exits into the backstage area, closing the door behind her. Pause.

PHIL: *off*   Tonight was just not in the cards, Peggy. I know it now. To have the critics predisposed against you is one thing. To have Providence, is quite another. I believe He's trying to tell us something. He's in this door, sweetheart. I believe that, within an inch of my life. The God of the Old Testament. "Vengeance is mine, sayeth the Lord." The world is torn by chaos and strife. Nation against nation. Race against race. Religion against religion. Critics against actors. My people created the theatre, bless their souls. Two thousand years ago. To celebrate the gods. To celebrate life. *What* is He trying to tell us here tonight? I wonder, I wonder. Is He telling us that we've strayed too far in the wrong direction? Telling us in His own inimitable fashion to get back to the celebration of life. If He is, Amen to that. Amen. Because, Peggy, the human spirit is sacred and holy, a shining light in all of us. Disregard the nay-sayers, the cynics, the philistines. The human spirit is alive and deserves to be uplifted and enshrined.

TOM stirs, sits up.

TOM: *groggily*   Phil, is that you?

PHIL: *off*   Yeah, I'm still here.

TOM: What're you doing? What was all that talk?

PHIL: *off*   Just getting into character, old buddy.
    I figured I might as well make use of the time.

*NICK bursts into the Green Room, carrying a toolbox
and axe.*

Blackout.

Music.

Act Three

The set of the play-within-the-play, the next afternoon around 1:30.

The stage still remains set for the last scene of the play from the previous night.

At rise, GEORGE and ROBERT are sitting at the table, working on the script, while PEGGY moves about setting up for the top of the play.

ROBERT: Page sixty-five. Jessica's first line. I think it's weak.

GEORGE: I like it.

ROBERT: Wouldn't it be more effective to say nothing? That would make Phil work harder to reach her.

GEORGE: *wearily*   Cut it, cut it.

ROBERT: Not unless you agree.

GEORGE: I agree, for Christ's sake.   *He strokes out the line.*   But if it doesn't work, I'm putting it back in.

ROBERT: Page seventy-three. Middle of the page. Patrick's second speech. . . . George, the line is, "I went *towards* her and she began to cry." That's much better than what he's been saying.

GEORGE: What's he been saying?

ROBERT: "I went *to* her and she began to cry."

GEORGE: "To" instead of "towards?"

ROBERT: The rhythm is better.

GEORGE: That might be tricky. He's gotten used to saying "to."

ROBERT: You mean changing a preposition is going to blow his performance?

GEORGE: No, but it won't make that much difference, either.

ROBERT: George, let a character use one word he wouldn't normally say and I stop believing him.

GEORGE: Listen, I've got to consider morale. If I keep harping on such minor points . . .

ROBERT: *cutting in*   Minor points?

GEORGE: Yes, minor points.

ROBERT: To you it may be minor; to me it makes me cringe in my seat. And don't you think you ought to tone down his performance? It was way too big last night. I'm surprised he never got slammed by the critics.

GEORGE: Robert, please. Look, I've got enough on my mind right now. Give me a break, will you?

He picks up his script and crosses to the sofa and sits, exasperated.

Just then, TOM rushes down the aisle. He carries a small brown paper bag containing a sandwich and coffee.

TOM: *thrusts the bag at GEORGE*   I'll never go to Luigi's again. That's the last time, George. He embarrassed me so much I went cross-eyed.

ROBERT: Cross-eyed?

TOM: Yeah, whenever I feel ridiculous I cross my eyes. You know, to unfocus the world.

GEORGE: Why? What happened?

TOM: He wanted my autograph.

GEORGE: *sipping his coffee*   Tom, you've just had your first taste of success. Learn to live with it. It's when they stop asking, you start to worry.

TOM: I don't mind autographs, George. I hate actors who treat their fans with contempt.

GEORGE: Why're you so upset then? I don't understand.

TOM: He had nothing to autograph, so you know what he gave me?

GEORGE: What?

TOM: You know what he gave me, George?

GEORGE: What did he give you?

TOM: A menu. Like, he took a menu off the table and had me sign it. He even told me what to say.

GEORGE: Well, to him it's a big deal. He'll take it home and show his kids.

TOM: No, he won't. He put it back on the table. George, I know dozens of people who go in there every day for lunch.

ROBERT: What did you write?

TOM: "Hugs and kisses from the world's greatest actor, Tom Kent." I'll never live it down, George!

He starts to exit.

GEORGE: Tom, wait a minute. Come here. I want to talk to you.

TOM returns.

GEORGE: Forget Luigi. Listen, what I'm about to tell you, I don't want you to mention it to Jess until I've told her myself. Okay?

TOM: *beat*   Bernie Feldman had a heart attack.

GEORGE: Worse. He went back to New York this morning. One of his shows is in trouble. The way things look he may not make it back before we close.

ROBERT: Two-faced little creep.

TOM: Who does he think he is, the President of the United States? Even the President can spare a night at the theatre.

GEORGE: I know.

110

TOM: Doesn't he realize how much this means to Jess? Doesn't he care how hurt she'll be?

GEORGE: I know, I know.

TOM: Bernie Maple Leaf Feldman. He comes up here as if he's doing us all a big favour, and then screws off.

ROBERT: Coitus interruptus.

TOM: He probably knocked up some showgirl and has to run back to get her an abortion.

GEORGE: I know, I know, I know.

TOM: Jesus, George. Jesus, Jesus, Jesus. *He starts to exit and turns.* Well, there goes my film career!

He exits backstage.

GEORGE: He's going to make a wonderful actor, that kid.

ROBERT: I know. He's got the right combination of empathy and self-absorption.

GEORGE: *to PEGGY* Are the others here yet, love?

PEGGY: It's only twenty-five after. They'll be trickling in soon. Robert, are you going to be long? I'll need you to move.

GEORGE: We're almost finished, Peg. Just say the word. *To ROBERT.* We *are* almost finished, aren't we?

ROBERT: One more and that's it. Page ninety-eight. Bottom of the page. Phil's line. We don't need the line. It's subtext. Phil can act it.

GEORGE: Great. His lines I don't mind cutting.

He strokes out the line.

ROBERT: He's been screwing it up anyway. Last night his excuse was he had a hair in his coffee.

Enter PATRICK down the aisle, carrying a small thermos bottle and cup. He looks slightly hungover.

PATRICK: *sipping from the cup*   I take back what I've always said about critics. We're finally getting a few discerning ones.

GEORGE: Congratulations. That was a helluva rave the *Star* gave you.

He indicates the newspaper on the coffee table.

PATRICK: So Susi tells me. I've not read it myself. I just crawled out of bed.   *He steps on stage.*   Hello, Robert. What're you up to? Don't tell me, you've rewritten the entire first act.

ROBERT: Have you really not read the reviews?

PATRICK: Listen, sometimes I don't read them till the run's over. No, I mean it. I don't like to gloat. Irish coffee, anyone?

GEORGE: Too early for me.

PATRICK: Don't blame you, mate, it's bitter. Maybe I put in too much coffee. Oh, well.   *He sits at the table.*   Speaking of last night, didn't you think that was a strange audience? A bit subdued? I think the house was papered with academics looking for Meaning. Either that or Nick's entire family was there.

GEORGE: I thought the audience was marvellous. Very attentive.

PATRICK: Attentive is fine for a funeral. For the theatre,
I prefer wildly enthusiastic. And did you notice what
happened to my only laugh in the play? Some old lady
coughed right on the punch line. I could've strangled her.

ROBERT: That was Phil's mother. She was chewing her
rosary beads.

PATRICK: I might've known. I notice she never coughed
once on *his* lines.   *GEORGE passes the newspaper to
PATRICK.*   That's it, is it?   *He begins to clean his
reading glasses.*   Too bad Feldman wasn't here last
night. He missed a good show. The cast was in top form. .

GEORGE: Listen Pat, about Feldman. . . .

*At that moment, NICK comes out from around the set and,
at the same time, SUSI starts down the aisle to the stage.*

NICK: Excuse me, George. I just did an equipment check.
The Christmas tree lights aren't working.

GEORGE: How long will you be?

NICK: A few minutes. It's probably the plug.

He sits in the window seat and repairs the plug.

SUSI: George, Phil just called from home. He said to tell
you he's just leaving. He might be a few minutes late.

GEORGE: We'll wait. I can't start without him. I need
all four actors.

SUSI: You'll never guess where he's been all morning.
At the hospital.

GEORGE: The hospital? Don't tell me his eye is worse?

SUSI: I was afraid to ask. I figured he'd never get off
the phone.

GEORGE: How did he sound?

SUSI: Hysterical.

PATRICK: Listen, he's at the hospital more than the doctors. He's on a first name basis down there. They set their watches by him.

SUSI: This was different. I've never heard him act so strange.

GEORGE: How do you mean?

SUSI: I could hear his mother in the background. And get this: he kept telling her to shut up and leave him alone.

GEORGE: Oh, Christ, they've pumped him full of sodium pentathol.

SUSI: It's out of character, isn't it? Let's hope he's not having a nervous breakdown.

She starts back up the aisle.

GEORGE: That woman's going to be the death of him yet, I swear.

SUSI: You think so? I have a hunch he'll get her first.

She exits.

PATRICK: *finds the review*   Don't you just love this? "*Roses* Author Has Green Thumb." Oh, that's cute. *To GEORGE.*   I don't know why, but I always expect to get knocked by this fellow.

GEORGE: Didn't you make a pass at his wife?

PATRICK: Maybe that's the reason. No, really. He always
     gives me a rave, but in each one he manages to get in
     these little digs. Remember *Murphy's Diamond*?
     "Mr. Flanagan plays the baseball coach with a lustful
     twinkle in his eye and the smirk and leer of a perverted
     Peter Pan." Okay, Patrick, settle down. Quiet on the
     set, please. The modest actor will now read his glowing
     good fortune, brief though it be. . . .   *Reads.*
     "Last night a remarkable new play burst on the scene
     at the small but prestigious Leicester Street Playhouse.
     Entitled *The Care and Treatment of Roses*, it is the
     much-awaited second play by Robert Ross, the young
     author of the highly successful *Murphy's Diamond*
     of three seasons past. The new work is old-fashioned
     in the true sense of the word: well-written and well-
     structured, observing at least two of the classical
     unities of place and action. The play spans three days
     in the lives of its characters, and the outcome is
     moving indeed."   *To GEORGE.*   I can see this
     is going to be boringly good. "Elizabeth Thompson
     (Jessica Logan), newly-widowed, has taken a lover
     (Patrick Flanagan), a violent and irascible bartender,
     a widower who is haunted by the spectre of his dead
     wife. With this simple situation the playwright weaves
     a seamless fabric of passion and renewed hope that
     threatens to unravel when her son, a college student,
     decides to remain at home during the winter break.
     He bitterly resents his mother's cohabitation with this
     man and is intent on destroying the relationship. He fails
     to understand her needs and the new lease on life that
     this vulgar opportunist symbolizes."   *To himself.*
     "Vulgar opportunist." Well, I suppose that's better
     than "perverted Peter Pan." "The play opens with
     Elizabeth and the lover, Frank, awaiting the arrival
     of her brother, Eric (Philip Mastorakis), a parish priest
     who has been summoned to persuade the son to remain
     in school. If there is a flaw in this play, it is simply that
     it begins too quickly. We leap at once into the conflict."

ROBERT: What does he want, Ibsen? Two maids telling
     each other things they already know?

PATRICK: "A more gradual build-up, it seems to me, would have worked much better."

ROBERT: The nit-picking is just to prove he's doing his job. He can't just come out and say it's perfect.

PATRICK: Right. "Enter the son (Tom Kent), the catalyst, who sets off the powder keg of conflicts. From the moment Mr. Kent staggers on stage, hung over from the previous night, the stage is set for a classic battle of wills, refereed by the priest — a battle that rages almost unrelentingly until the final curtain." *To himself.* Ah, now comes the good bit. "The cast for the most part is superb. Patrick Flanagan as Frank, in the most impressive performance of his career, gives a tone and texture to his character that is truly breathtaking. There is not a false note in it. His final reconciliation with Elizabeth in the last moments of the play is the most genuinely moving moment of the night." *To GEORGE.* I thought I was better in the last preview, didn't you? "Tom Kent in the pivotal role of the son, Jimmy, manages to strike the right balance between awkward youth and groping aspirations. A fine debut for a young actor in his first professional role." *To GEORGE.* Oh, that should please Tom. I'm glad he got that. "But by far the most memorable performance of the night ... *He pauses, his expression turning from incredulity to outrage.* ... goes to Philip Mastorakis as the priest, brother of the much-put-upon Elizabeth." *To GEORGE.* The most memorable performance of the night! We carried him the whole night, the three of us. *He tosses the newspaper to GEORGE.* Here, you read it. I can't read that garbage.

GEORGE: *reads* "But by far the most memorable ..."

PATRICK: *cutting in* Must you repeat that? That's only one man's opinion, remember?

116

GEORGE: "In a brilliant stroke the playwright has paralleled and contrasted the groping of the son against the loss of faith of this most human of all priests."

PATRICK: He was so out of it before we went on I had to remind him to check his fly.

GEORGE: "Mr. Mastorakis, vulnerable in an almost painfully child-like manner, fumbling for words that seem constantly to elude his grasp, makes the inner struggle seem all the more urgent and adds a dimension of humanity that endears him instantly to the audience."

PATRICK: You sure his mother never wrote that?

GEORGE: "The only disappointment in the cast is Jessica Logan as the doleful Elizabeth."

PATRICK: You're kidding.

GEORGE: No, he hated her.

PATRICK: She was wonderful. No, I mean it. I wouldn't say that to her face, mind you. Christ, and he liked Mastorakis. Well, that just proves what I've been saying all along about critics. By the way, what does he mean, "the doleful Elizabeth?"

ROBERT: Melancholy.

PATRICK: That'll piss her off. All along she thought she was archetypal. What else does he say?

GEORGE: "Perhaps Miss Logan has been absent from the theatre too long. Perhaps she misjudged the intimacy of the small theatre. The fact remains that her performance is by far too large for such an intimate space, almost wildly extravagant, reducing the character at times to caricature. She starts off at such a high emotional pitch she has nowhere to go except into the upper ranges of hysteria."

PATRICK: God, that's terrible. She'll be devastated.

Slight pause.

NICK: *still working on the plug*   Don't stop there, George. Read the rest.

GEORGE: "For this, the director, George Ellsworth, must in part be faulted, although, otherwise, his handling of the cast is exemplary. Mr. Ellsworth has demonstrated in the past . . ."

PATRICK: *cutting in*   Don't tell me. "A fine and delicate touch."

GEORGE: ". . . a fine and delicate touch, an unobtrusiveness that is the hallmark of a first-rate director. Perhaps Miss Logan was simply too strong a personality to control. That aside, *The Care and Treatment of Roses*, quite simply, is the best new play to arrive all season. And if it does not become the hottest ticket in town, this reviewer for one will eat his hat."

He tosses the newspaper on the coffee table.

PATRICK: Eat camel dung.

PEGGY: Typical. He didn't mention the set, costumes, or lighting.

GEORGE: *to PATRICK*   The other papers are in the front office. You want to read them?

PATRICK: What do they say?

GEORGE: Basically the same thing.

PATRICK: The answer is no. And to think I crawled out of bed for *that*.

He crosses to the armchair with his thermos bottle and cup. He picks up a magazine and begins to leaf through it noisily.

PEGGY: George, I'm almost through. I need the table now.

GEORGE: It's all yours, Peg. And thanks.   *He crosses to the table with his script.*   Robert, give it a rest. Peg needs the table.

ROBERT: I can take a hint.

GEORGE: Why don't you use my office? Type some of these pages.   *He hands ROBERT his script.*   Only don't fuss with my desk. I like disorder. I'll never find a thing if you straighten up.

ROBERT: Yeah, well, that clutter drives me crazy. At home I can't even work if the bed's not made.

He exits up the aisle.

GEORGE sits down on the sofa and sips his coffee.

PATRICK: *turning pages*   Phil Mastorakis?

GEORGE: I know. That should throw him into a tailspin. He's grown to expect the worst.

PATRICK: I thought he was much better in *Titus Andronicus.*

GEORGE: Are you serious? He was *dreadful* in that.

PATRICK: I know.

Enter JESSICA from backstage. She is bristling. As she strides on, she is swinging her wig. PATRICK buries his face in the magazine, and NICK, who is on his feet checking the Christmas tree lights, darts back into the window seat and pretends to be fixing the plug.

JESSICA: Where's George? Ah, there you are. Stand up. I want a word with you.

GEORGE: How are you, love? What can I . . . ?

JESSICA: *cutting in* Have you been in the dressing room this morning? I use the term loosely. Black Hole of Calcutta's more like it. Even my roses wilted.

GEORGE: What's wrong with the dressing room?

JESSICA: What's wrong? It *reeks* back there, that's what's wrong. The wallpaper's starting to peel from the smell of popcorn and cigarettes.

GEORGE: Popcorn?

JESSICA: Yes, popcorn. I know what popcorn smells like. Like a roomful of dirty socks. I defy anyone to go back there and not gag. Poor Tommy is face down on the sofa muttering, "Jesus, Jesus, Jesus."

PEGGY: *to GEORGE* I haven't cleaned it yet. I was just about . . .

JESSICA: *cutting in — to GEORGE* What do you take us for, a pack of degenerates? As if it wasn't bad enough before, being herded into a sweatbox, now you deny us a door on the WC. It's disgraceful.

GEORGE: Nick, hasn't that door been replaced?

JESSICA: No, it has not. Are you calling me a liar? And I want a fan back there to circulate the dust. You have one in *your* office, I notice.

GEORGE: *to PEGGY* Leave that for now. Clean the dressing room. Get someone to repair the door. And bring down the fan from my office. Right away.

PEGGY exits quickly backstage.

JESSICA: *to GEORGE*   Don't look at me like that.
I won't be pitied or patronized. These are legitimate
complaints, not the whimsy of some delinquent child.

GEORGE: Sorry, love. I wasn't aware that I . . .

JESSICA: *cutting in — she brandishes the wig*   And I won't
wear this one more night, do you understand? Would you
wear it? No, you're goddamn right you wouldn't. Yet you
have the nerve to dress me up in a wig that any little
street tart would think in bad taste. Well, I won't wear it.
She tosses it to him.   Take it back to the zoo where
you found it. I play a housewife in this play, not Harpo
Marx in drag.   *She turns and strides over to PATRICK
and knocks away his magazine.*   And don't you ever
hang up on me again, you hear? Don't you *ever*!

PATRICK: Was that you this morning? I thought it was
an obscene call.

JESSICA: You're just lucky you took the phone off.

PATRICK: Had I known it was you, love, I wouldn't
have been that rude. I don't have any real friends. Only
fans and enemies.

JESSICA: *starts to exit*   If I were a man, I'd take
you outside and pummel you.

PATRICK: If you were a man, I wouldn't go.

JESSICA: Coward!

She exits.

PATRICK: A rather weak exit line, I thought. Even
Robert can do better.

GEORGE: *to NICK*   Why the hell wasn't the door put
back on the washroom?

NICK: The reason it wasn't put back yet is because we weren't supposed to have this illegal rehearsal, that's why.

GEORGE: This rehearsal is not illegal.

NICK: According to the Equity rulebook we need twenty-four hours to call a rehearsal after an opening.

GEORGE: *angrily*   You know what I'd like to do with your Equity rulebook?   *He tosses the wig to NICK.* The same thing I'd like to do with your friggin' callboard.

JESSICA comes storming back on. NICK exits quickly around the side of the set.

JESSICA: *to GEORGE*   I suppose you think I'm being a bitch, don't you? Just because I demand to be treated like a human being.

GEORGE: Jess, I don't think you're a bitch. I don't think that at all.

JESSICA: Well, I am a bitch, and you know why? I have to be to get treated like a human being. So there.

GEORGE: I see your point.

JESSICA: What point?

GEORGE: About being a bitch.

JESSICA: So you think I'm a bitch, do you?

GEORGE: No, no . . .

JESSICA: *cutting in*   I knew you did.

GEORGE: No, I meant demanding.

JESSICA: Oh, really?

GEORGE: Yes, I think you're demanding.

JESSICA: Why? Because I demand to be treated fairly?

GEORGE: No, because . . . *He pauses.* Jess, I think I'm lost. . . .

JESSICA: What was I saying?

GEORGE: Don't you know?

JESSICA: Did you change the subject?

GEORGE: What was it?

JESSICA: I don't remember. . . .

She sits on the arm of the sofa and lights a cigarette, looking very fragile and wounded.

PATRICK: *rises* Excuse me, I have to call my agent. I'm the only one who ever does. It cheers him up.

He exits up the aisle.

Pause.

JESSICA: Oh, George, I have the mark of Cain on me. In this racket that's worse than leprosy and twice as contagious. Aren't you worried you'll catch it?

GEORGE: Listen to me. You're not a failure. Far from it. You bring more humanity to this part than any actress I know. You're just finding your level, that's all.

JESSICA: *paces* What's the circulation of the *Toronto Star*? You have any idea?

GEORGE: Half a million?

JESSICA: That many? Oh, God, it's worse than I thought. Half a million people who don't know my work now believe Jessica Logan to be "wildly extravagant."

GEORGE: Jess, you were the one who asked for this rehearsal. Didn't you say last night you thought you were too big?

JESSICA: It's one thing for *me* to say it, it's quite another to wake up in the morning and find it in print.

GEORGE: I think you're overreacting.

JESSICA: Yes, you can afford to be generous. They all *loved* you.

GEORGE: What do you care about one or two critics? The audience adored you. They gave you a standing ovation.

JESSICA: Be serious. They gave *us* a standing ovation. Besides, most of that audience was made up of relatives and well-wishers. They still hadn't read the papers to find out what they were supposed to think.

GEORGE: That's a bit cynical, isn't it?

JESSICA: I'm feeling cynical. My own brother saw the show and raved about me. This morning I showed him the *Star* review. You know what he said? "I didn't think you were *that* bad." George, I wasn't that bad, was I?

GEORGE: You have never been bad in your life.

JESSICA: To be the only one singled out. And to be drawn and quartered so brutally. "She has nowhere to go except into the upper ranges of hysteria." Anyone who didn't know better would think it was an opera.

GEORGE: Jess, listen to me. The phone hasn't stopped ringing. The answering service is threatening to raise our rates.

JESSICA: I'm not surprised. Opera is very popular.

GEORGE: This show could be the biggest hit we ever had. We're already sold out for the next three days.

JESSICA: Oh, how he must be gloating, that little pig, that slug. Do you know what I find so contemptible? The pomposity, the incredible arrogance. I thought only the Pope was infallible; at least with the Pope it's a Divine Right.

GEORGE: Forget what he said, will you? Don't take that garbage so seriously. You're too good for that.

JESSICA: I don't take it seriously, George, and I don't give a damn *what* he thinks. It still hurts. We spend weeks and months on a play to be carved up by someone on a free pass who rushes home to scribble off six or seven hundred words in sixty minutes that affects our livelihood and reputation. I don't know about you, but I can't even write a letter in that length of time. And oh, his writing style, let's not forget that. He writes like he needs a good enema. His sentences are so tight-assed, if he ever left out a period he'd run right into Classified Ads.

GEORGE: That's all the more reason not to take him so seriously. Who in his right mind would want to be praised by that man?

PATRICK: *off* Phil Mastorakis.

JESSICA: *to GEORGE* He's been eavesdropping. *As PATRICK comes down the aisle.* I thought you were calling your agent.

PATRICK: The phones in the office are busy.

JESSICA: Well, don't you disparage Phil. At least he has
     respect for his fellow actors. He'd never deliberately
     make someone look bad.

PATRICK: *steps on stage*   I agree. By comparison
     he makes us look better.

ROBERT starts down the aisle.

JESSICA: Is that why you got raves?

PATRICK: Which makes me wonder why you didn't.
     Maybe in New York you should play the Met.

Pause.

JESSICA: *quietly*   That's it. I quit. I quit, I quit,
     I quit.

GEORGE: You quit? . . .

JESSICA: As of right now. You have my resignation.
     Effective this very second.

*ROBERT sits on the edge of the stage and puts his head
in his hands.*

GEORGE: *in a panic*   Could we clear the theatre,
     please? Everybody out in the lobby. I want to talk to
     Jess alone.

JESSICA: Save your breath. I don't intend to work
     with someone whose tongue is sharper than his wit.
     Out of my way, Flanagan. I'm in a very dangerous
     mood.

*PATRICK steps quickly out of her path as she exits
backstage.*

GEORGE: Dammitt!   *Then.*   What're you doing
     here, Robert? Why aren't you up in the office?

ROBERT: It's your wife, George. She just called from the hospital. She asked me to give you a message.

GEORGE: *angrily*   What does she want now?

ROBERT: A visit.

GEORGE: Can't you see what's happened? I'm busy. I'll see her tomorrow.

He hurries backstage.

ROBERT: *yells after him*   That's it for me! I'm writing novels!

He steps on stage and sits on the sofa and taps his foot.

Pause.

PATRICK: What're you trying to say, Robert? Get it off your chest. I never did learn morse code.   *Pause.* So I'm the villain of the piece, am I? Is that it? Well, don't forget: I made you what you are, you little bugger.

Pause. PATRICK sits at the table.

PATRICK: I was only kidding. I don't know why I even said it. I'm just talking to hear myself. I've never liked being alone.   *Pause.*   How's your new play coming? You got a title yet?   *Pause.*   Funny you should mention it, but I've been meaning to ask about *The Care and Treatment of Roses*. What precisely is the difference between "Care" and "Treatment?   *Pause.* Listen, she was just looking for a way out. You know that, don't you?

ROBERT: Then why'd you give her one? Jesus, you're an actor. You know how vulnerable she is right now.

Pause.

PATRICK: What'd you stop for? You have more to say
when I leave out a comma. Give me hell if you want.
I know you hate my guts.   *Pause.*   Listen, where do
you get off blaming me? I'm the one who should be
angry here. I'm the one she used.

ROBERT: You?

PATRICK: She baited me. You heard her. All I did was
react like any good actor. Goddamn prima donna.
I can act circles around her or anyone else in this
country.

ROBERT: Is that why you stay here?

PATRICK: Just what does that mean? On second thought,
keep your mouth shut. I don't like what comes out.
He stands and begins to exit.   And if you think
you're such hot stuff, maybe New York's just what you
need.

ROBERT: Maybe it is.

PATRICK: *turns back to ROBERT*   How would you
like to find out you're not as good as you think you are?
As good as everyone says? Can you take that? Having
your nose rubbed in your own worse doubts about
yourself?

ROBERT: I'm not afraid of it, if that's what you mean.
He turns to face PATRICK.   Listen, I want that
experience. I want to be put up against the best.
Otherwise, how am I going to grow, Flanagan? How
do I develop?

*Just then, JESSICA comes storming back on, carrying her
make-up kit. Desperately, GEORGE runs ahead of her.*

JESSICA: No, I've taken all I care to take from that
imbecile. I won't demean myself further. So goodbye.

She attempts to leave the stage but GEORGE blocks her way.

GEORGE: Jess, wait, wait. Let's not be rash. I know you're upset, but can't we all sit down and discuss this like adults?

JESSICA: We're not adults, we're actors. If you haven't learned that yet, you have no business in the theatre. Now get out of my way.

GEORGE: Jess, without you in the cast this show will fall apart. I could never find a replacement.

JESSICA: That's not true. I can think of any number of actresses who could do this part and better.

GEORGE: Name one.

JESSICA: Offhand I can't, but that's beside the point.

GEORGE: Jess, this part was *made* for you. Robert practically wrote it with you in mind. Didn't you, Robert?

ROBERT: Practically.

JESSICA: *indicating PATRICK*   I can't work with that man. He's the worst excuse for a human being that I've ever run across.

PATRICK: *to ROBERT*   I'll let that one go by.

JESSICA: He's had my stomach in knots from day one. Oh, I can forgive his ill-manners and his ill-temper. I can forgive his vicious sense of humour. I can even forgive his alcoholic phone calls and his caravan of pizza trucks.

PATRICK: How am I doing, Robert?

JESSICA: But what I can't forgive is unprofessionalism. His behaviour last night on this stage was nothing short of atrocious.

PATRICK: *angrily* And what was that, may I ask? Unless you're referring to my damn fine performance. In which case I stand justly accused.

JESSICA: And you attack Robert for being ironic. My God, if that isn't ironic.

PATRICK: How was I unprofessional?

JESSICA: *crossing so that she, too, is upstage of the table* You know damn well what I'm talking about. *She sets her make-up kit on the table.* From the moment you strutted down those stairs you pulled out every stop. You snorted and bellowed like a wounded moose.

PATRICK: I did like hell! *To GEORGE.* Did I? . . .

GEORGE turns and walks up the aisle.

PATRICK: *to GEORGE* I know I was rushing, but . . .

JESSICA: *cutting in* Rushing? You were *charging*. The rest of us could barely keep up.

PATRICK: Look, it was opening night. We were all nervous. Anyway, it's your own fault. You're the one who invited Feldman up here.

JESSICA: He wasn't in the audience.

PATRICK: Did I know that? Every time I looked out I thought I saw him glowering. So maybe I was bigger than usual. A touch.

JESSICA: Bigger?

PATRICK: Must you repeat every word I say?

JESSICA: The word is shrill. Shrill as in frightened silly.
Shrill as in Irish soprano. And in half those scenes I'm
supposed to top you.

PATRICK: If we were both shrill, then how come only
you got panned?

JESSICA: Because I am the star, darling. I am the
goddamn star of this show, and don't you ever forget it!

*TOM rushes on from backstage. He sees what he thinks is
the "apron" scene being rehearsed.*

TOM: Sorry, George. I fell asleep. You want me to get
the apron?

GEORGE: I don't think so, Tom. And I don't need you,
either. We haven't started yet.

TOM: Oh. I thought. . . . Like, I thought . . . you
know. . . .

GEORGE: I know, I know.

PATRICK: *to JESSICA*   Go ahead, tell the kid why
there won't be a show tonight. I think he deserves an
explanation. And don't use me as a scapegoat.

TOM: There's no show? . . .

PATRICK: Your mother just quit.

JESSICA: I'm sorry, Tommy.

PATRICK: The papers'll say, "For reasons of health."
But we all know the real reason, don't we?

GEORGE: *from up in the aisle*   That's enough, Patrick.
Stop it.

PATRICK: *to GEORGE* Then why didn't she quit last night? Why did she wait for the reviews? And why walk out the same day as Feldman is coming? Answer me that.

JESSICA: Stop badgering him. What do you think this is, *Inherit the Wind*?

GEORGE: Forget Feldman, the both of you. He's not coming tonight. He's gone back to New York. And good riddance.

PATRICK: What? . . .

JESSICA: I don't believe it. . . .

GEORGE: It's true. Ask Robert. Some crisis came up and he left.

ROBERT: He has no class, either. He left the message with the answering service.

JESSICA: *to GEORGE* Was this before or after the reviews came out?

GEORGE: *runs down onto the stage* Jess, for God's sake, stop believing the critics!

JESSICA: Well, I don't believe that excuse, either. He just didn't want to face me, the coward. After all, I'm supposed to be the draw in New York and I was the only one who got panned. He can hardly take it there now, can he?

GEORGE: That's his tough luck. We'll take it there without him. I just don't want you believing you were bad.

JESSICA: Bad? I was dreadful last night, and you know it. Godawful.

GEORGE: You were not godawful, you were wonderful. All we have to do now is get it back to the right size, and that goes for Patrick as well.

PATRICK: Me?

GEORGE: *firmly* Yes, you!

Enter NICK down the aisle. He can barely suppress his indignation. He puts one foot on the stage.

NICK: Excuse me, George. I'd like to speak to the cast, if I may. Well, may I?

GEORGE: Oh, be my guest.

NICK: *steps on stage* Now I'm not accusing anyone, I want you all to understand that. But someone in this theatre has taken a hammer and ripped the callboard off the stairwell.

JESSICA: Someone stole the callboard? *She laughs.* Oh, God, there is a God after all. Wait'll I tell Phil.

NICK: I'm sorry, Jessica, but I fail to see the humour. That callboard is there for a purpose. I want it replaced.

JESSICA: Well, I'd like to take the credit. Believe me, I would.

NICK: I'm not accusing you. I'm just saying I want it nailed back up by eight o'clock tonight.

JESSICA: Don't you take that tone with us. You're lucky we don't nail *you* to the wall. Now trot back to the control booth and pull in your horns.

NICK: Don't tell me what to do. You're no longer with this show.

JESSICA: *crosses slowly to NICK*   Listen, you, I have never walked out of a show in my life. The day I decide to let down my fellow actors I guarantee you will be the first to know. Now stop wasting our time. We've got a rehearsal to get through.

She looks over at GEORGE.

GEORGE: *pause*   Well, you heard the lady. We'll be starting as soon as Phil arrives.

NICK: Eight o'clock, George, or find yourself another stage manager.   *He starts up the aisle and turns.*   And I resent being made an ogre!

He exits.

GEORGE: *crosses and hugs JESSICA*   Thanks, Jess.

JESSICA: God love the sonofabitch who stole that callboard.   *She glances at ROBERT, then at TOM, who shakes his head vigorously. Slight pause.*   Thank you, Flanagan.

PATRICK: Me?

JESSICA: It was you, wasn't it? Who else is perverse enough to think of it, let alone do it?

PHIL rushes down the aisle. His eye is swollen and badly discoloured. He is wearing an ascot, a beret and Hawaiian shirt.

PHIL: I'm sorry, boys and girls. I got here as fast as I could.

GEORGE: How are you? How'd it go at the hospital?

JESSICA: The hospital?

PHIL: *stepping on stage* Ah, friends, you don't know what I've been through. No possible idea. I can't begin to describe it. Sheer torture.

PATRICK: What were you doing, paying a bill?

PHIL: That's exactly what I'd expect from you. No, I wasn't paying a bill. I was getting my stomach pumped.

JESSICA: What!

PHIL: *nods grimly to the others* Incredible, huh? Fantastic.

GEORGE: Are you serious?

PHIL: Would I kid about a thing like that? You ever had your stomach pumped? It's murder.

JESSICA: No wonder you're pale. That must've been an ordeal.

PHIL: Tubes down the throat, needles, the works. I figured I was a goner. Food poisoning.

TOM: Food poisoning?

GEORGE: How'd you get that?

PHIL: George, that's not the worst of it. I just buried my cat, Gus.

GEORGE: Gus is dead?

PHIL: May he rest in peace.

PATRICK: Let me get this straight. You ate your cat?

PHIL: Very funny. No, my cat ate the tuna salad.

PATRICK: Then who ate your cat?

PHIL: Nobody ate the cat. What's wrong with you? Don't you ever listen?

JESSICA: Phil, start from the beginning. We'll unravel it together.

She sits him in a chair at the table.

PHIL: Okay. This's what happened. It's early this morning. Around seven. My cat's making noises. A wonderful cat. Like a brother. He's into the medicine chest, knocking pills in the sink.

PATRICK: Does he do that often?

PHIL: Every morning. That's how he gets me up. Intelligent, huh? I hurry down to the kitchen. I hunt around. No cat food. Nothing in the fridge but a bowl of tuna salad my mother made. I give Gus some and make myself two toasted tuna salad sandwiches on rye. To keep him company. Okay, he's finished. I put him outside on the porch and go back to bed. Around nine I get up, make myself coffee, and go out to get Gus. *He chokes up.* There he is, George. He's lying stretched out on the porch. . . .

GEORGE: Dead?

PHIL: Stiff as a board.

JESSICA: Darling, I'm sorry.

PHIL: I panic. My first thought: food poisoning. I call an ambulance and in no time I'm at the hospital. The rest you know.

JESSICA: Phil, that's terrible. What a trying day.

PHIL: You think that's bad? Wait till you hear the finish. I go home. I'm depressed, wiped out. My mother comes back from shopping. "Oh, Phil, Phil," she says, "I'm so miserable." "You think you're miserable?" I say. "Yes, I'm wretched. I have a terrible confession to make. This morning I backed out the driveway and ran over Gus. I didn't want to ruin your sleep so I put him on the porch." *He shakes his head incredulously.* And she wonders why I'm mad.

PATRICK: Phil, do you ever feel that life is making you the butt of some vast practical joke?

PHIL: Hey, what're you trying to do, make me paranoid?

PEGGY enters and continues her preset of the table.

JESSICA: Yes, you leave my Phil alone. He got the best notices in the show. Didn't you, my heart?

PHIL: I was fortunate. Very fortunate, I must say. And what they said about you, Jessica, is disgusting. I intend to write a letter to the editor. Better still, I'll cancel my subscription to the *Star*.

JESSICA: That's sweet of you, darling, but let's not get drastic. I'll tell you what you can do, though. Be brilliant tonight. We'll all be brilliant. To hell with Bernie Feldman.

NICK: *over the P.A. — his voice sharp with anger* George, the rehearsal was called for two o'clock. It's now 2:05.

GEORGE: *to the cast* Okay, let's settle down. This'll only take a minute. What we'll do today is start from the top. We'll run each scene individually and then work on it.

TOM: Costumes?

GEORGE: No, just props. I also want to work some light and sound cues. Does anyone object to that? No? Okay, then let's get this show on the road.

NICK: *over the P.A.* Top of Act One in two minutes, please.

JESSICA: *taking TOM's arm* Your mother doesn't have to wear her funny hair. Isn't that good news?

They both exit backstage.

PHIL: George, I've been thinking. Maybe I should go back to the hairpiece.

PATRICK: George, if Phil's getting his rug back, I want my adjustable lighter.

He exits.

PHIL: George, can I have tinted glasses for tonight? It doesn't look right, George, a priest with a black eye.

He exits.

ROBERT: *rises from the sofa* What about the changes?

GEORGE: Later. We'll work them in during the run. Now is not the time.

He starts up the aisle.

PEGGY: *to the control booth* I'm all set, Nick.

She exits.

ROBERT: What's your opinion, George? You think this play could make it in New York?

GEORGE: If not this play, Robert, your next. You've got your whole life ahead of you.

NICK: *over the P.A.*   He hasn't got that long. He has exactly sixty seconds unless he gets the hell off my stage.

ROBERT starts up the aisle as PHIL rushes back on stage.

PHIL: George, what's this I hear about Feldman? Are they kidding me or what?

GEORGE: *from his seat*   I'm afraid not, Phil.

The lights begin to dim and the music starts.

PHIL: Beautiful. Just beautiful. The best reviews of my life and nothing will happen.

GEORGE: Phil.

PHIL: George, Feldman was my only hope: he was an American. Down there they embrace success. Up here it's like stepping out of line.

GEORGE: Phil, get off the stage.

PHIL looks crushed. He starts to exit. The lights are still dimming.

GEORGE: Hey, Phil.

PHIL stops and looks out at GEORGE.

GEORGE: Just remember: he's not the only producer in New York.

PHIL: I know, but he was single and the right age.
     I thought I had my mother all lined up.

Blackout.

Music.